JANET TODD is a novelist, biographer and literary critic. A former President of Lucy Cavendish College, Cambridge, she is an internationally renowned scholar and academic, known for her work on women's writing and feminism. Her most recent publications include *Radiation Diaries: Cancer, Memory and Fragments of a Life in Words*; *A Man of Genius*; *Lady Susan Plays the Game*; and *Aphra Behn: A Secret Life*. She is the General Editor of *The Cambridge Works of Jane Austen* and editor of the *Cambridge Companion to 'Pride and Prejudice'*.

convincing in its blend of confession, quirkiness, humour, intimacy. It's nothing short of a literary masterpiece, inventing a genre. A delight too is the embeddedness of books in the character of a lifelong reader; it is fascinating to learn of Todd's fascinating variegated past. How gallant (like the verbal gallop against mortality at the close of *The Waves*)' Lyndall Gordon

'Beautifully written, viscerally honest, horribly funny' Miriam Margolyes

'A quirky, darkly mischievous novel about love, obsession and the burden of charisma, played out against the backdrop of Venice's watery, decadent glory' Sarah Dunant

'Strange and haunting, a gothic novel with a modern consciousness' Philippa Gregory

'A mesmerizing story of love and obsession in nineteenth-century Venice: dark and utterly compelling' Natasha Solomons

'Intriguing, pacy and above all entertaining; clever, beguiling' Salley Vickers

'Genuinely original' Antonia Fraser

'A rip-roaring read' Michèle Roberts, *Sunday Times*

'Terrific insight. Todd's sound and generous reimagining of women's lives is a splendid work' *Publishers Weekly (Starred)*

'Mesmerizing and haunting pages from a Gothic-driven imagination' *Times Literary Supplement*

'Gripping, original, with abundant thrills, spills and revelations' *The Lady*

Recent works by Janet Todd

The Cambridge Companion to 'Pride and Prejudice' (editor)
(Cambridge: Cambridge University Press, 2013)

Jane Austen: Her Life, Her Times, Her Novels
(London: André Deutsch, 2014)

Lady Susan Plays the Game
(London: Bloomsbury, eBook, 2013; paperback, 2016)

A Man of Genius
(London: Bitter Lemon Press, 2016)

Aphra Behn: A Secret Life
(London: Fentum Press, 2017)

Radiation Diaries: Cancer, Memory and Fragments of a Life in Words
(London: Fentum Press, 2018)

Jane Austen's
Sanditon

With an Introductory Essay

by

Janet Todd

Fentum
Press

Fentum Press, London

Sold and distributed by Global Book Sales/Macmillan Distribution
and in North America by Consortium Book Sales and Distribution, Inc. part
of the Ingram Content Group

Introductory Essay and revised text copyright © 2019 Janet Todd

Janet Todd asserts the moral right to be identified as
the author of this work

A CIP catalogue record for this book is available
from the British Library

ISBN (paperback) 978-1-909572-21-8
ISBN (EBook) 978-1-909572-22-5

Typeset by Lindsay Nash
Printed and bound in Great Britain by TJ Press

Jane Austen's *Sanditon*

Table of Contents

Introductory Essay

The two faces of Jane Austen: the watercolour sketch by her sister Cassandra; and its prettified version to accompany her nephew's hagiographical Memoir *in 1870*

The phenomenon of Jane Austen

Jane Austen is one of the greatest novelists in English Literature, a pioneer in fiction and an immense influence on those who wrote after her. Whether intended for publication or private amusement, whether from finished or abandoned works or from fragments, all her words have interest for us now in our eclectic and curious twenty-first century.

Her fame rests primarily on the six published novels. With a first glance, these appear simple, romantic, almost wish-fulfilling tales. Yet, each is profoundly complex, and each is distinct in tone and technique. Few people fail to be delighted by a first reading of *Pride and Prejudice* or *Persuasion;* further readings of *all* the novels reveal the delights of unexpected intricacy, meaning, subversion – and sometimes uncomfortable conformity to values now largely ignored. The greatness of Jane Austen is that her books are never exhausted; they retain an ability to nudge and surprise.

Reading is a conversation between novelist and reader, and each generation reads Jane Austen differently, finding her speaking to cultural concerns hardly glimpsed by readers in previous centuries. And we ourselves may read her several times over the years: when we do, we find her

3

addressing our new interests, while she lets us bring something from our own stage of life to an interpretation of her protean works.

Austen is that rarity in the traditional canon of English fiction: a figure pored over by scholars while being loved and read by the general public. Only Dickens and the Brontës come close to this achievement, but not even those valued writers have acquired her megafandom, leading to an internet full of invented characters snatched from the novels to become psychotherapists, detectives, etiquette gurus and teenaged pals. Jane Austen's books have been subjected to analysis in all facets, while films and television adaptations have made the author and her fiction a global brand.

Happily, she has survived fame and celebrity unspoilt.

The popularity is explicable. Love and romance are winning subjects and Jane Austen delivers them, but with a hard-headedness about money and compromise that surprises a reader who comes from the films to the novels rather than vice versa. The characters she creates seem real: they live in families with whom they must relate, however repugnant some of the members, as well as in the wider society of men and women. Her heroines learn how to stay true to their own intelligence and some inner core of being, while coping with uncongenial people and responding to constricting social pressures. They are believable.

Yet Jane Austen and the characters she creates move in a

world very different from ours. The early nineteenth century is often called Regency, although the actual Regency, when George III was declared insane and unable to govern, lasts only from 1811 to 1820. It occurs just before the railways made England smaller and its people more mobile, and before photography became widespread, causing us to look back on the Victorian world as predominantly black and white. Jane Austen has become synonymous with a colourful Regency of romance and grace. In popular culture she also stands for heritage, an immemorial rural England of church, great house and grateful villagers, a place of stability.

In fact, the Regency was a time of extraordinary upheaval and change. It included two revolutions, the effects of which are still being worked out in the modern world. The French Revolution started in 1789 when Jane was still a child, then morphed into the first truly global conflict, the Napoleonic Wars, lasting, with one brief interval of peace, until 1815 and darkening almost all Jane Austen's adult life. The Industrial Revolution, which would transform Britain into the first urban industrial power, accelerated in her lifetime, ultimately reshaping the world.

Readers have remarked that Jane Austen's subject ('3 or 4 Families in a Country Village') seems largely to ignore these turbulent historical events, as well as the movement of enclosure which turned England into a land of private property and hedged fields. (Austen's own family members benefited from this transformation.) But look closely and you will catch between lines and in apparently desultory dialogue glimpses of all these changes. You will also encounter political and social opinions sometimes gratifyingly liberal, at others sternly alien to our present way of thinking: rare certainties and many ambiguities.

Her life

Jane Austen was born on 16 December 1775 in Steventon, a small village in Hampshire. Her extended family was mixed, including a few rich landowners, many clerics, and an apprentice milliner. Hers was a reasonably pleasant middle-class background, close to the gentry but never absolutely secure in status or income.

Her father George Austen, a country rector, obtained his living through patronage of a wealthy relative, and augmented it with farming and tutoring pupils for university. He had need of all the income he could get, for he and his wife Cassandra had eight children to raise. Two were girls, Jane and her elder sister Cassandra.

Apart from a disabled one, the boys did reasonably well in life through patronage and effort. The eldest James followed his father into the Steventon living. Edward, the most fortunate, was adopted by rich relatives called Knight, and in due course inherited their vast estates which included Godmersham Park in Kent and Chawton House in

Hampshire. At the tender ages of eleven and twelve, Frank and Charles entered the Royal Naval Academy and rose up the ranks during the long French wars. Henry became soldier, banker and clergyman by turns.

In contrast, the Austen girls had marriage or attendance on relatives to look forward to in later life. Both received marriage proposals. Cassandra was engaged to a curate who became a military chaplain and died abroad, while Jane accepted, then speedily rejected, an offer from a neighbour, Harris Bigg-Wither, a young man of good family and estate but insufficient attractions. Perhaps, too, she already knew what she wanted most of all to do with her life. It was not long after this rejection that she sold her first novel – *Susan* – though sadly it was not printed at the time. (It was revised and came out posthumously as *Northanger Abbey*.)

Jane began writing early, amusing her family with comic, knowing little stories and plays, then turning her hand to complete novels. First versions of *Northanger Abbey*, *Sense and Sensibility* and *Pride and Prejudice* were all composed at the rectory in Steventon. Then, abruptly in 1801, youth ended. Her father decided to leave his son James as curate of Steventon and move to Bath where he and his wife could take the waters for their health. Unconsulted, the spinster daughters of course accompanied them.

Soon after the move, in 1805, George Austen died, and his income with him. For the next years the Austen women led a makeshift life, moving from place to place to be near male relatives or find suitably cheap lodgings. Finally, in 1809, they were rescued by the wealthy Edward, who set up his mother and sisters in a former bailiff's cottage on his estate in Chawton. From this house, Jane published her first novels, *Sense and Sensibility* and *Pride and Prejudice*. Then followed two new ones, *Mansfield Park* and *Emma*, both evoking a more intense sense of home than the books drafted in Steventon. After she died, two further novels, the early drafted *Northanger Abbey* and the late *Persuasion* were brought out by her family.

On her death at the age of only forty-one, Jane Austen left two works unfinished. *The Watsons* was begun in the Bath years. It tells the story of a family of girls rather like

The cottage in Chawton, Hampshire

the Bennets, but the work lacks the lightness and jollity that make *Pride and Prejudice* so appealing. The Watson daughters need to marry but from more desperate financial circumstances. As the heroine remarks to a stupid, rich young aristocrat, 'Female economy will do a great deal my Lord, but it cannot turn a small income into a large one.'

Jane Austen made many corrections and revisions to the manuscript, then stopped writing. Possibly the difficult situation of the women she described came too close to her own rather insecure life; possibly her existence in all its facets was simply interrupted by her father's death. The novel was to have depicted the death of a clergyman, who dies leaving his daughters unprovided for.

The other, more fluent, innovative fragment is *Sanditon*. The writing of this was not abandoned but interrupted by her own last illness, which ended in her death in July 1817.

Sanditon *and its plot*

Was there ever a fragment like it? The distinguished novelist suffering a long decline – her brother Henry alleged that 'the symptoms of a decay, deep and incurable, began to show themselves in the commencement of 1816' – used her last months to compose a work that mocks energetic hypochondriacs and departs radically from the increasing emphasis on the interior life marking the previous novels. However weak her body – and she wrote some passages first in pencil, being unable to cope with a pen – clearly her spirit was robust. Not only that: worrying herself sick about money after a family bankruptcy, she was writing a book of jokes about risky investments and comic speculators.

For us, her readers and admirers, the farcical, ebullient *Sanditon* is achingly sad, for it ends with 'March 18', neatly written on an almost empty page. The final date signified that Jane Austen would write no more novels. A few days later she admitted, 'Sickness is a dangerous Indulgence at my time of Life.' She had begun the work in a period of remission, but now she sighed, 'I must not depend upon being ever very blooming again.' In April, she admitted, 'I have really been too unwell the last fortnight to write anything': she was suffering from 'a Bilious attack, attended with a good deal of fever'. Four months after interrupting her last novel, she died.

Frugal with paper and densely covering her page with neat handwriting, at her death she left empty a large portion of the homemade *Sanditon* booklets (created by folding and cutting sheets of writing paper, then stitching them together). *We* know that she was dying, she could not be sure. As a result of these blank prepared pages, the final dating, and the enigmatic nature of the plot, what is not written haunts what is, and no number of continuations by cameras and other pens can quite displace the ghostly presence of that emptiness.

In contrast to the earlier novels about great houses and

fine constantly occupied by Sir H. D.
March 18.

The final, mainly empty page of Sanditon.

rural villages, *Sanditon*'s twelve chapters do not describe a tight country society but a developing coastal resort full of restless travelling people – the novel becomes an exuberant comedy not of organic community but rather of bodies whose weaknesses are delivered with zest. It is a surprising subject for Jane Austen's last work, which fits neither with her previous subtle comedies of manners nor with the sentimental romantic nostalgia they gave rise to in her global fandom. The world of *Sanditon* is absurd, unsettled and unsettling.

The fragment introduces an array of smart, silly and ludicrous characters. Like *Northanger Abbey* and *Mansfield Park*, it begins by translating the heroine, Charlotte Heywood, to a place where she can enter a story. She is the first Austen heroine with the name (although Elizabeth Bennet's friend Charlotte Lucas plays a significant role in *Pride and Prejudice*). In a letter of 1813 Austen related how she met a 'Charlotte Williams', whose sagacity and taste she admired. 'Those large, dark eyes always judge well. – I will compliment her, by naming a Heroine after her.'

Charlotte Heywood's translation comes about through an accident. On his way from London to the coast and making a detour to find a surgeon for his new resort, the impetuous Mr Tom Parker unwisely insists on trundling his hired coach up a poorly maintained lane. It overturns, and the crash gives him a sprained ankle. He is forced to stay with nearby rural landowners, the practical Heywoods,

'The Runaway Coach', Thomas Rowlandson, c. 1791

just then busy with June hay-making; on his departure, he repays their fortnight's hospitality by carrying with him one of their fourteen children.

Unlike the heroines of *Northanger Abbey* and *Mansfield Park*, Charlotte is not deposited in a great house to cope with bullying or tyrannical inmates. Instead, she is taken to the new resort of Sanditon on the Sussex coast, where, much like her fictional predecessors, she will, over the next weeks, observe, judge, maybe change and possibly find love – though by the end of the fragment few hints of a lover are emerging beyond a promising mention of sense and wealth in Tom Parker's younger brother Sidney. (Perhaps strangely so for readers eager to find romance in the author herself. A family tradition has Jane falling in love in the Devon coastal resort of Sidmouth, probably with a clergyman – the younger family members often seem eager to provide male love-objects for their famous aunt. The absence of letters from 1801 to 1804 when she visited five or more resorts shrouds the possible romance from biographers – but not from creative fans.)

In her role as observer, the clear-eyed Charlotte less resembles the usual Austen heroine who matures through incidents and errors and more the foreigner or stranger used in satire to notice and comment on eccentric and perplexing native habits – or Lewis Carroll's young, down-to-earth Alice trying to assess Wonderland with above-land tools. An older, more mature narrator bustles in at times to stress Charlotte's inexperience and tendency to categorical judgement – a narrator far from the 'impersonal', 'inscrutable' one Virginia Woolf discovered in Austen's work. A young woman of Charlotte's age quite properly appreciates sexual interest and should enjoy the attentions of a handsome baronet, remarks the narrator. But mostly she lets us see through her heroine's youthfully disapproving, sometimes intemperate eyes, so that we are led to laugh at a proliferation of herbal teas or a cautious consideration of butchers' meat and servants' wages, without hesitating to wonder if this is wise.

Jane Austen had just been revising her old novel *Northanger Abbey* when she began *Sanditon*. In her character as judge and observer, Charlotte is almost the reverse of the earlier heroine since she assumes rationality in the irrational, where Catherine Morland does the opposite. The people whom Charlotte mostly watches are not young men and women competing for marriage partners but the speculating pair behind the resort's creation: her host, the enthusiastic Mr Parker, and Lady Denham, the local great lady with 'many thousands a year to bequeath' and three sets of relatives courting her. Parsimonious and mean, she is also, like so many women in Austen's novels, cannier in money matters than the men around her.

Among the arriving visitors to Sanditon are Tom Parker's siblings, two vigorously invalid sisters and a third brother, the indolent, guzzling Arthur, who has caught the habit of ill health like an infection from his sisters. With gusto the trio self-diagnose and self-medicate, and together they form a droll commentary on the new leisure pursuit of hypochondria and invalidism which the eldest brother Tom Parker is exploiting.

Plot incident is promised through the circle of toadies round Lady Denham. These include two rivals for the widow's unusually disposable property: the impecunious heir and nephew by marriage, Sir Edward, the 'remnant' of a second husband, and Clara, a distant relative chosen over nearer kin to be Lady Denham's companion.

The usual assumption was that quixotic girls (like Catherine Morland of *Northanger Abbey*, and Lydia Languish

'Mixing a Recipe for Corns', George Cruikshank, 1819

in Sheridan's *The Rivals* and Arabella in Charlotte Lennox's *The Female Quixote* before her) were most susceptible to fiction, but, from her juvenile tales through to *Sanditon*, Jane Austen knew men were just as likely to be overwhelmed. In *Love and Freindship*, written when she was fourteen, Sir Edward discovers his son, another Edward, has a head filled with 'unmeaning Gibberish' from sentimental novels, while a second Sir Edward in *Sanditon* is addled by sensational romance (Austen was a frequent recycler of names and motifs). Both young Edwards are prey to precisely the kind of fiction she herself does not write but towards which some of her less acute supporters tried to steer her by suggesting more 'incident'. In *Sanditon*, Sir Edward intends to provide 'incident' by being what Austen termed 'a very fine villain'. Misreading and misusing literature, he proposes to be a charismatic rake in the line of Lovelace, who rapes the virtuous heroine in Samuel Richardson's huge tragic novel *Clarissa* of 1748, surely an outdated libertine model for a young man of 1817 when the most celebrated society seducer would have been Lord Byron – although Byron rarely needed Lovelace's violence.

To fulfil his wicked ambition, Sir Edward proposes to abduct the beautiful Clara out of the clutches of Lady Denham. He fancies a solitary house near Timbuctoo to

Illustration depicting Lovelace molesting Clarissa

take her to – in fact all he has on offer is his own damp property and the tourist cottage he is building on Lady Denham's waste ground. The fragment trails off before Sir Edward can act or Clara can resist.

Charlotte thinks Sir Edward 'downright silly', though he is not alone in seeing Clara Brereton through the gauze of literary melodrama or gothic: Charlotte too refers to Clara as a 'character' and a 'heroine' in a story. The put-upon 'humble companion' was a stock figure of female novels of the time and, with her beauty, poverty and dependence, Clara seems to Charlotte ripe for such a literary role.

Beyond any single person, in *Sanditon* the seaside resort is subject and centre of the novel – and Mr Tom Parker is almost synonymous with it:

> Sanditon was a second wife and four children to him — hardly less dear — and certainly more engross-ing. — He could talk of it for ever. — It had indeed the highest claims; — not only those of birth place, property, and home, — it was his mine, his lottery, his speculation and his hobby horse; his occupation, his hope and his futurity.

It has invaded his mind so that he can boast with crazy sincerity that its sea air and bathing are 'healing, soft[en]-ing, relaxing — fortifying and bracing — seemingly just as was wanted — sometimes one, sometimes the other.'

An Austen family tradition has as the intended title of the fragment not the seaside resort itself but 'The Brothers'. The suggestion has some merit since, as far as the twelve chapters can tell us, the three Parker brothers, Tom, Sidney and Arthur, will form interesting contrasts throughout the story. Such a masculine title and such a dominant theme of male relationships would, however, be as much a break with the six complete novels as the comically exaggerated characters appear to be.

Jane Austen does describe close relationships between men – Darcy and Bingley in *Pride and Prejudice*, the Knightley brothers in *Emma* – but she doesn't much dwell on them and there are far more depictions of women together, especially sisters when these are congenial.

In her life too, outside the hazy heterosexual romances, Jane Austen reveals close ties with women, her sister Cassandra of course, but also with cheerful, kindly Martha Lloyd, called 'friend & Sister', with whom, she, Cassandra and their mother lived most of the time from 1805 until Jane's death; the Bigg sisters, the lifelong friendship with whom survived the debacle of Jane's one-night engagement to their brother Harris Bigg-Wither; her two eldest nieces, Fanny Knight and Anna Austen; and two women below her own gentlewoman status, Anne Sharp, Fanny's often ailing governess at Godmersham – her 'sweet flattery' of Jane's writing success made her 'an excellent kind friend' – and Madame Bigeon, a French emigrée and Henry Austen's housekeeper, to whom she left £50 in her will. In the fragment of *Sanditon*, the most intriguing female relationship is that between the poor companion Clara Brereton and the patroness Lady Denham.

Within Jane Austen's immediate family there are also close relationships between Jane and her five brothers, though they differ in intimacy. It is least evident with Edward, the most distant in circumstance and place – the only one whose name is used in the novel (for the predatory baronet) – most with Henry, of whom there are more descriptions in her surviving letters. With the eldest James, she shared a love of reading and writing, and she had huge respect and affection for Frank and Charles and fascination for their adventurous naval careers. In *Sanditon*, whatever might have been intended for the finished novel, in the part we have the dominant family players are not the three brothers but the enthusiastic, addicted brother-and-sister pair, Tom and Diana Parker. If the work should be named after family members at all, it might perhaps best be titled 'The enthusiasts: Thomas and Diana Parker'.

Both siblings are mocked for this enthusiasm, and also for their shared desire to surround themselves with company. Although sociable, especially in her last years Jane Austen relished periods of solitude, times when she was 'very little plagued with visitors', when she might enjoy 'quiet, & exemption from the Thought & contrivances which any sort of company gives'. Tom and Diana are eager for company of all sorts at all times, Diana imagining and scheming for visitors and Tom Parker seeing the whole of Sanditon as a kind of house party, only successful if crammed – he had wanted to bring *all* the Heywoods with him to Trafalgar House. In this he is heir to Sir John Middleton in *Sense and Sensibility* and Mr Weston in *Emma*, whose desire for company frequently exceeds that of their more discerning guests.

For a fictional plot to develop, however, a houseful of guests and frequent comings and goings have many advantages.

Jane Austen in Sanditon

If the grotesque portraiture of the twelve chapters differs from the characterisation in the mature novels, it has much in common with that in the wacky, clever and surreal little tales the child Jane wrote to delight her family in the Steventon rectory, amusing them by using their names in stories and dedications. In fact, her enthusiasm for rollicking humour and parody did not end with childhood; a compulsive bent, it surfaced throughout her life in her private writings. It is expressed in shared literary spoofs, comic poems, and often in intimate letters. The fiction she wrote in her last housebound months may in part be intended, like her juvenile writings, to amuse her family.

None of Jane Austen's mature heroines quite resembles

her creator, though each reflects some of her qualities: her wit and moral temperament, for example, as well as her social circumstances. With her sceptical approach to life, yet her enjoyment of fiction, *Sanditon*'s Charlotte Heywood may seem close to aspects of Jane Austen, but she is too undeveloped – and perhaps prim – for much identification.

A more bizarre but closer fit is Mr Parker's spinster sister, Diana, much given to the imaginative and leisure activity of heroic invalidism. Austen mocks her mercilessly, quoting at length the garrulous account she writes to her brother cataloguing her and her siblings' sufferings and her deluded, energetic do-gooding, which Charlotte terms 'Activity run mad'. But Diana also has her author's doggedness, her resilience and brilliance at fantasy, an ability to remake herself and the world around her, whatever the setback; she is allowed to rattle on and wander from topic to topic rather as Jane Austen herself often does in her intimate letters, and she, like Jane, lives in Hampshire. Chillingly, E. M. Forster, the novelist and great admirer of Jane Austen's finished work, suggested the resemblance when he compared the writer of *Sanditon* to a 'slightly tiresome spinster, who has talked too much in the past to be silent unaided'.

Jane Austen's nephew and first lengthy biographer, James Edward Austen-Leigh, was dismayed by his aunt's surviving letters when he read them; he found them trifling. Charlotte too, contrary to Mr Parker's expectation, is not charmed by Diana's desultory epistolary style. Yet Jane Austen knew that most of the business of keeping separated families together depended on women sending letters, written whether or not there were any exciting incidents to report. In *Northanger Abbey* Henry Tilney pretends gallantly to support female superiority in letter-writing, while, more sincerely, Mr Parker is grateful to his sister Diana for writing often, when his brother Sidney does not.

Despite roundly mocking her, Jane Austen shares ailments with her character. Diana Parker's 'old grievance, spasmodic bile', is close to her creator's: just before beginning *Sanditon*, Jane wrote, 'I am more & more convinced that *Bile* is at the bottom of all I have suffered, which makes it easy to know how to treat myself.' To her list of supposed medical jargon in *Sanditon*, 'anti-spasmodic, anti-pulmonary, anti-septic, anti-bilious and anti-rheumatic', the term 'anti-bilious' was added later. Diana moaned that she could 'hardly crawl from her bed to the sofa': Jane Austen admitted she was now 'chiefly on the sofa'.

Perhaps the vigour with which the hypochondriacal Diana Parker conquers her bilious disorder is a wish fulfil-ment of the truly sick Jane Austen (equally wish-fulfilling might be her comfortable situation, for Diana is well-provided for where her author is not). Also, mocking bodily infirmity, even if chiefly imaginary, might have helped Jane herself ward off any tendency to self-pity and petulance:

'generally speaking it is [human nature's] weakness and not its strength that appears in a sick chamber,' she noted in *Persuasion*.

Outside fiction, Jane Austen found the hypochondriac more irritating than comic. She described a distant relative as 'the sort of woman who gives me the idea of being determined never to be well – & who likes her spasms & nervousness & the consequence they give her, better than anything else'. Nearer home, she may have found another example of hypochondria: reading between the lines, we might hear occasional exasperation with her mother and her 'complication of disorders', about which she was rarely silent. Mrs Austen survived her daughter by a decade.

Jane Austen's robust attitude to her own health or sickness, her tendency to believe in the remedies of brisk walking and rhubarb, made her sometimes unsympathetic to other sufferers. Her friend Anne Sharp experienced dreadful migraines and eye problems; unlike Jane, she sought extreme and new-fangled medical cures, including a painful suture in the nape of her neck, electrodes to her head and the cutting off of all her hair. Possibly she persisted because she knew that continued ill health would ruin her modest job prospects – doubting her friend's fantasy that she might marry a relative of her rich employer. Herself ailing by 1816, Jane Austen was irritated into sarcasm by Anne's frequent complaints of ill health and naïve optimism about people and cures: 'she has been again obliged to exert herself more than ever – in a more distressing, more harassed state – & has met with another excellent old Physician & his Wife, with every virtue under Heaven who takes to her & cures her from pure Love & Benevolence . . .' Sympathy returned, and Jane wrote her last letter from Chawton to her 'dearest Anne', saying farewell and describing with 'all the Egotism of an Invalid' her own appalling symptoms.

Beyond ill health, Diana Parker echoes her creator by being a house-hunter. Following her father's death, Jane, Cassandra and their mother began a nomadic life, primarily dependent on the brothers for income, moving from lodgings to ever cheaper lodgings in Bath – then for a while staying with brother Frank and his family in Southampton, a port and spa (in Jane's childhood writings notable for its 'Stinking fish'). Until they came to live in Chawton in 1809 with Edward's help, they had no settled home. A search for a home is one of the perennial themes of all the novels and it is an irony of her subsequent reputation that in later years Jane Austen was regarded as pre-eminently the novelist of stability and home. But not even Edward was secure and, when Jane was writing *Sanditon*, he was suffering a lawsuit which threw doubt on his claim to his huge estates, one of which included the Chawton cottage.

Diana Parker is not homeless, but she is consumed by finding lodgings for what turn out to be mythical visitors, and her manic house-hunting may draw something from

Jane Austen's experiences of trudging round Bath looking at 'putrifying Houses' in the hope of finding a place they could afford. All the novels are obsessed with houses, but none mentions so many kinds as *Sanditon*, which becomes a veritable estate agency of a book with its terraces, tourist cottages, hotels and puffed lodging-houses – all in imagination filled with rich tenants.

Underpinning anxiety about homelessness is of course money. Here the author's life presses most fiercely on *Sanditon*. Jane Austen was not only disturbed by Edward's threatening lawsuit but by something more definite. It happened just after she finished the last sentence of *Sanditon*, but it likely contributed to her inability to take up her pen again, so leaving her fragment 'upon the Shelve' along with *Northanger Abbey*.

Mrs Austen's rich brother James Leigh-Perrot and his wife Jane were childless, and it was always understood that his estate in due course would come to his sister's children but that, if his death preceded his wife's, there would be immediate legacies for the needy Austens. Eleven days after Jane Austen stopped writing *Sanditon*, Thomas Leigh-Perrot died. To the great disappointment of the Austens, he left everything to his wife for her lifetime – and this despite their standing by her during the murky incident when she was accused of shoplifting and faced transportation for the crime. 'I am ashamed to say that the shock of my Uncle's Will brought on a relapse,' Jane wrote. 'I am the only one of the Legatees who has been so silly, but a weak Body must excuse weak Nerves.'

If she were indeed suffering from Addison's disease, as many suppose, this added stress would have been hugely detrimental; she herself was aware that 'agitation' could be as harmful as fatigue. Possibly in the portrait of Lady Denham and her treatment of her poorer relatives, there was something of the whimsical and mean selfishness Jane Austen saw in aunt Jane Leigh-Perrot. (A modern critic, straying into gothic mode, finds Lady Denham an early example of the childless 'rich lesbian vampire', who collects husbands and property and preys on sick or poor young women.)

One of the reasons for Thomas's decision – unmentioned by Jane Austen – may well have been the Leigh-Perrots' anger at losing a large sum of money through the bankruptcy of Jane's speculating banker brother, Henry Austen.

Henry and Jane

Henry benefited mightily from the long Napoleonic Wars. At first intended for the Church like his eldest brother James, he had instead joined the local militia, soon becoming paymaster and agent. He resigned his commission in 1801 and set up business as a banker in London, partnering local banks in Kent and Hampshire, one in the market town of Alton, very close to Chawton. He was also connected to small country banks in a couple of speculative inland spas: Buxton in Derbyshire and Horwood Well Spa in Somerset. The wartime economy helped all his projects with its huge defence spending as well as import restrictions which kept agricultural prices high – advancing the interests of his main customers, the landowners, though not of the urban or rural poor.

Jane was pleased at the prosperity enjoyed by her charming, witty and sanguine brother. She admired, loved and indulged him, rejoicing at his successes and sympathising in his setbacks. She stayed often with him in London, where one of his lodgings was above his bank in Henrietta Street. There she met his lively friends and colleagues and witnessed his financial activities. She attended the theatre with him and even came to the notice of the Prince Regent – whom she heartily despised. Hearing that Henry had been invited to the season's most desirable social event in 1814, the ball at White's Club celebrating the (temporary) allied triumph over Napoleon, she exclaimed, 'O what a Henry!'

Yet, for all her supportiveness and admiration, she would have been painfully aware that as a woman she had none of Henry's opportunities to increase her own modest income. Perhaps in this respect Lady Denham with her own money and speculating choices is wish-fulfilling, rather like Diana Parker with her conquerable sickness and private income.

In one area of course Jane could enter the marketplace: through her writing, though not easily without male support. Henry advocated his sister's work, made connections with publishers and saw her novels through the press. With his help she speculated in publication by not selling most of her copyrights outright, the unfortunate exception being *Pride and Prejudice*, which would have brought her most money. She loved the 'pewter' she earned: 'I have written myself into £250 which only makes me long for more,' she wrote. Just after she penned the last words of *Sanditon*, she received nearly £20 for the second edition of *Sense and Sensibility*. It gave her a 'fine flow of Literary Ardour'.

But her earnings were always modest. Especially unfortunate was the decision not to sell copyrights of her later novels to her final publisher John Murray: as a result, she earned little from *Emma*, since the losses on *Mansfield Park*'s second edition were set against its profits. It had not been a successful speculation.

In 1815 the battle of Waterloo ended the Napoleonic Wars and England was at peace for the first time in twenty-two years. After initial rejoicing and jollity came inevitable disappointment. The effect of peace on the economy was huge: financial and social adjustment, even depression, wracked the country. Through Henry, Jane now had first-hand experience of market volatility: his wartime prosperity was over. In 1815 the Alton bank was already struggling: it collapsed in March 1816. The rest of Henry's businesses failed in a welter of debts. He lost his home and possessions and was declared bankrupt.

Henry Austen as Rector

With her other siblings, Jane showed no distaste at Henry's murkier dealings, for patronage, nepotism and dependence on the great were part of the family background. Little blame seems to have been cast on the always charming brother, though he took his family down with him. Especially hit were Edward and uncle James Leigh-Perrot, the first owing £20,000 and the second £10,000. Jane herself lost £26. 2s, part of the profits from her writing. After their father's death, the Austen brothers had clubbed together to provide a small income for their sisters and mother. After the crash, little of this could be paid.

Despite such huge losses, Henry's optimism and vitality were undimmed. He returned to his original life-plan and took Holy Orders. Jane Austen was impressed by his resilience, a quality she gave in spades to her speculator Mr Parker.

Can speculative capitalism be good?

Jane Austen wrote *Sanditon* in the winter and spring following the famous dark summer of 1816. Away in Switzerland under the gloom, Mary Shelley invented her monster and Byron his vampire. The pall over Europe was caused by the eruption of Mount Tambora more than 7000 miles away. The volcano spewed out gas and particles that hid the sun; temperatures dropped, crops were blighted. Hunger was widespread.

In England landowners who had flourished under wartime protectionism made the situation worse by banding together to pass corn laws against cheap imports, ignoring the principle of free trade and the needs of a hungry population. No accident that the poor who come to the attention of Tom and Diana Parker required subscriptions from the better-off to keep afloat.

Jane Austen's characters are all in various ways defined by money. Indeed, her novels' tendency to dwell on the economic side of life startled the poet W.H. Auden, who described them in his poem as revealing

> so frankly and with such sobriety
> The economic basis of society.
>
> 'Letter to Lord Byron'

In her fiction we learn that the dowager has her jointure, the widow her allowance, the heir his expectations, the rich girls their dowries, the poor their scrambling needs, the warriors their prizes and the peacetime officers their half pay. We know who is landed and who funded by means of investments in government stock, and whose fortune comes from trade or an ancestor's clever speculation. In short, we know what most characters are worth.

There is much to spend on. *Emma* displays a traditional economy whose basic commodities are produced locally and circulated: apples and the hind-quarter of a pig travel from the wealthy to the poor, and gifts of meat, fruit and craft are exchanged among equals. Yet there are also particulars of fashionable and leisure items brought in from outside the region. These come to the fore in *Sanditon*; added to which, even the most necessary foodstuff is here bought and sold for money. Once self-sufficient from his own estate, Mr Parker now *pays* for much of the produce and meat he needs in this new commercial economy.

Regency England was afloat with consumer goods through 'the demand for everything', as Mr Parker puts it. Fictional Sanditon, like the real seaside resorts, was full not only of new and unfinished buildings but of all manner of expensive things that marked status and answered whims: dresses, lace, straw hats, shoes, fancy boots, bonnets, gloves, books, camp stools, harps and carriages. The whole town is for sale and to let, and visitors are consumers who

Etching by Thomas Rowlandson from
Poetical Sketches of Scarborough, *1813*

must make it flourish – Charlotte feels obliged to buy something when she enters the local subscription library and trinket shop which sells 'all the useless things in the world that could not be done without'.

Even people may become saleable items: Sidney Parker, the most dashing of the Parker siblings, is a useful attraction for displaying girls and their scheming mothers. The rich 'half mulatto' Miss Lambe, an heiress from the West Indies, is desirable as both a paying visitor and as prey for one of the town's needy bachelors – such as Sir Edward.

Glorious British victories of the Napoleonic Wars were speedily commercialised – war tourism to Waterloo was established almost before the dead were cold; their bones were collected and sold as souvenirs. The names of battles dwindled from being patriotic achievements to become adornments, embellishing new houses, terraces and squares of peaceful England. By 1817, the naval battle of Trafalgar, which had meant so much to Jane Austen through her sailor brothers, had lost cultural, even decorative, cachet through relentless exploitation. It had been replaced by the more recent Waterloo, the bubble of whose fame would likely be popped long before Mr Parker was dead. As it is, he regrets that, just a year before Waterloo, he had named his new property Trafalgar House and saw it become almost instantly out-of-date.

Although four of the complete novels – viz *Sense and Sensibility*, *Pride and Prejudice*, *Mansfield Park* and *Persuasion* – have financial mismanagement at their core, uniquely in *Sanditon* the topic of national economy is widely discussed, as it was throughout England in these years. Debates raged in pamphlets and books, in taverns and private homes, concerning profit and loss, capital and property, wealth and paper credit.

In his pioneering work of capitalist theory, *The Wealth of Nations*, Adam Smith stressed the idea that the pursuit of self-interest can benefit society generally. Yet many doubted that the greed and extravagance of the rich would benefit those below them, that wealth inevitably trickled down and that capitalist activity and consumption were good for all. Satires noted that the extravagant and dissolute lifestyle of the Prince Regent in his elaborate pavilion

James Gillray, 'John Bull ground down', 1795

in Brighton failed to improve the lot of the town's deprived inhabitants.

Other debates concerned speculation and types of capitalism. Can what is now called neoliberalism work for everyone in society or will it benefit only the few? Is speculation inevitably precarious? Is profit alone ever a worthy motive? Would the country prosper most under a *laissez-faire* system or should there always be welfare and paternalistic controls, so that development does not despoil an organic community? How does the constant need to buy new things, to enjoy purchasing then throwing away, impact on society and its traditional crafts? How does consumption affect morality? Under the urge to buy and sell, will the country dwindle into tourist haunts and shopping malls?

The Empire too was controversial. Was the home economy skewed by wealth coming from the colonies or was the Empire a drain on the Mother Country?

The characters in *Sanditon* debate these questions from their differing social positions – though they resemble each other in all being well-to-do. The traditional, stay-at-home landowner Mr Heywood (who however has his London investments paying 'dividends') is kind and welcoming to a stranger of his class, but he keeps the lower orders in their place. He leaves lanes beyond his house unpatched and his tenant cottages, pretty enough on the outside, unmodernised. Change erodes class divisions, he believes, and disturbs the tested ways of the past. The new resorts are bad for everyone because they cause inflation: they raise prices and 'make the poor good for nothing'.

Mr Parker, the traveller and projector, disagrees with this reactionary view. He accepts the working of the market place: it may disturb the old order, turning traditional fishermen and farmers into commercial sellers, but the new economy in the long run will benefit all. He believes in what Adam Smith had termed 'the invisible hand', that capitalist activity can benefit all. When the rich spend, they 'excite the industry of the poor and diffuse comfort and improvement among them'. Rich and poor are symbiotic: butchers, bakers and traders cannot prosper without 'bringing prosperity to *us*'. In many respects, however, Mr Parker remains an old-fashioned gentleman and his capitalism is tempered. The rich have a duty to support the unfortunate poor, and he cares for and patronises his unsuccessful traders as once he cared for the tenants on his estate.

His partner, 'mean-spirited' Lady Denham, sides with Mr Heywood, wanting to retain the privilege, status and security of the old order. In her sitting room, Sir Harry Denham, baronet, has a full portrait in pride of place over the mantelpiece, while the untitled but moneyed Mr Hollis is present only in miniature. At the same time, she supports Mr Parker through greed, being avid for the spoils of the new order. Like Mr Heywood, she worries about inflation, believing that visitors raise prices of local produce. Propelled by 'calculation' and desire for instant profit, she opposes any move of Mr Parker's that does not instantly bring in money or which has indirect consequences. A doctor in town would not simply attract invalids but also let servants and the poor fancy themselves ill. As Charlotte primly comments, Lady Denham degrades and makes mean those who depend on her – much like the inconstant and rich Mrs Ferrars in *Sense and Sensibility*.

Where did Jane Austen stand in the debate on speculation? The answer would depend on what fate she was proposing for Tom Parker of Sanditon. Perhaps he was heading for a crash, ominously foreshadowed in the opening pages by his overturned carriage. The very name of

Sanditon recalls Jesus's parable of the builders, in which the wise man builds a house on rock and the foolish one on sand, only to see it swept away by wind and water. The Parkers in their cliff-hugging Trafalgar House have already been rocked by storms unfelt in the valley. In the context of Jane Austen's Anglican world view, it might have been better if Mr Parker had been seeking a parson for his unstable new town rather than a surgeon when he insisted on pushing his hired horses up the treacherous road in Willesden.

The two previous books Jane Austen wrote, *Persuasion* and *Emma*, both concern landowners and stewardship and subtly connect them with national stability. Given the criticism of *Persuasion*'s Sir Walter Eliot as a poor landlord who lets out his ancestral home, and praise for Mr Knightley, the good, traditional one in *Emma*, it might seem that Mr Parker, who has abandoned and rented out his family estate, set like Donwell Abbey in a sheltered valley ('a hole' Mr Parker calls it with ominous disrespect), is in the line of spendthrift Sir Walter.

Without a conclusive ending, where ideological clarity is often found and subversive tendencies summarily reined in, we cannot be certain. Perhaps Mr Parker is not intended as simply the butt of conservative satire. His energy is attractive, and the real sense of change and new order that blows through fresh and sparkling Sanditon makes Jane Austen's view equivocal. The wind buffeting the cliff-top houses and deterring the timid lifts the spirits of those energetic enough to brave it – and, in *Persuasion*, similar sea wind restores bloom to the cheeks of drooping Anne Elliot. Although nothing suggests financial success for Sanditon, if Mr Parker does face a crash, perhaps he might be helped by his individually solvent siblings, especially the wealthy Sidney – rather than taking them down with him, as Henry had done his family. If Jane's beloved brother is pressing against the character, it is hard to imagine generous, open-hearted and reckless Tom Parker quite humbled or condemned for his delusions.

The passion for salt water

The British love affair with sea cures began in earnest in 1753 with Dr Richard Russel's *A Dissertation on the Use of Sea-Water in the Diseases of the Glands*. Believing in nature

as the best healer, it claims that sea bathing eases stiff joints and helps against tuberculosis, leprosy, venereal diseases and ulcers. Sea water has the healing qualities of 'Saltness', 'Bitterness','Nitrosity' and 'Oilyness'.

By 'bathing' is not meant 'swimming', especially enjoyed by men and boys, but 'dipping' for a minute or two in the cold sea water from a horse-drawn wooden box or machine. This dipping for health was undertaken by both sexes, especially if they were 'lax fibred'. For ladies, the box had a canvas modesty hood to avoid anyone seeing the bather. The contraption cost a shilling to hire and was trundled, rather uncomfortably, into the sea. Inside the box, the lady – a gentleman could dip in the nude – changed from ordinary clothes into a flannel bathing costume, attended by a 'dipper' who might well be fierce in 'helping' her patient put her body into the freezingly cold sea to 'charge the system'.

From mid-century on, claims for sea bathing accelerated: Dr Robert Squirrel declared it efficacious for 'Indigestion, Gout, Fever, Jaundice, Dropsy, Haemorrhages, Violent Evacuations, or any other disorder', while 'inspiring' or breathing sea air recovered health more than breathing anywhere inland. The literature dwelt on miracles. A Mr Sanguinetta, paralysed from the head down, took regular dips at Margate, then 'threw away his second crutch, and walked with a cane, took up his German flute and played'. He fathered seven children.

Coloured etching by William Heath, c. 1829

Nearer home, Jane Austen's glamorous cousin Eliza de Feuillide, future wife of Henry Austen, carried her ailing young son to Margate for a cure in December and January, having been told that 'one month's bathing at this time of the Year was more efficacious than six at any other'. Remarkably, the child survived: 'The Sea has strengthened him wonderfully & I think has likewise been of great service to myself, I still continue bathing notwithstanding the severity of the Weather & Frost & Snow which is I think somewhat courageous.' Although it is summer in Sanditon, delicate Miss Lambe from the West Indies will still find the sea immensely cold when she finally goes through the box into the water, with vigorous Diana Parker beside her to 'keep up her spirits'.

After half a century of seaside puffing, some medical men tried to moderate the fantastic claims for sea water. In *A View of the Nervous Temperament*, Dr Thomas Trotter mocked doctors who exploited illness for their own gain. Sea bathing, he wrote, was primarily 'an exercise and amusement', good perhaps only for nerves. Mrs Bennet, literature's most famous possessor of nerves, believes she would be 'set up with a little sea bathing' in Brighton.

The supremely healthy Charlotte Heywood agrees with Dr Trotter: she enjoys sparkling Sanditon but has no need for any ailment, and by the end of the fragment has not tried sea bathing. Robust Lady Denham avoids doctors, blaming them for killing off her second husband, and is

An engraving by R. and D. Havell from an original
by George Walker: bathing at Bridlington, 1813

never rhapsodic about the sea. She too of course wants to benefit from sickness in others: offering her remedies of asses' milk and an exercise chamber horse left over from her first husband.

Indeed, almost everyone in Sanditon aims to profit from the invalid or healthy body. Mr Parker seeks a doctor as a tourist attraction for his seaside resort, though, unlike Lady Denham, he does believe in the therapeutic value of sea air and bathing: he expects good breathing and 'immersion' to put him to rights after his carriage accident. Visiting Mrs Griffith, allowing modest sea bathing for her richest young lady, prescribes only those pills and drops in which a cousin

'Venus Bathing in Margate' attributed to Thomas Rowlandson.
Nude swimming was in fact very uncommon for ladies

has a commercial interest. In poems and puffing medical manuals, medicinal sea bathing could even sound useful for seduction; albeit praising the waters of the Hudson River, Samuel Low declared that 'the fair from thy embrace more lively shall retire/And that which cools their own, their lovers' breasts shall fire!' Had the manuscript been longer, perhaps the egregious Sir Edward would have had time to find amorous profit from female bathing, and tune his compliments accordingly.

The seaside resort

Today, with so many rundown resorts around the coast of England, it is tempting to glamorise the earlier quaint fishing-village with its heroic night fishermen and welcoming wives in tidy cottages, and grow nostalgic for an older way of life – the sort epitomised for the upper orders by the stay-at-home Heywoods. The poet William Cowper, a favourite author of Jane Austen's, looked on the new developments through conservative eyes. He believed such jumped-up places ruined old crafts through a fashion for novelty, making visitors prey to shoddy amusement, to morbid restlessness and to quacks:

> But now alike, gay widow, virgin, wife,
> Ingenious to diversify dull life,
> In coaches, chaises, caravans, and hoys,

> Fly to the coast for daily, nightly joys.
> And all impatient of dry land, agree
> With one consent to rush into the sea.
> from 'Retirement'

Contemplating the mushrooming sea resorts, the reforming journalist William Cobbett drily remarked that they had no commerce or agriculture, no purpose beyond catering for migrants' pleasure and so were 'very pretty to *behold*; but dismal to think of' – all metaphorically built on shifting sand, all sanditons. The money to sustain them must derive from outside, from other parts of Britain or from the Empire. More sustained ridicule came from Thomas Skinner Surr: in *The Magic of Wealth* (1815), he described a rich banker Flimflam creating 'Flimflam-town' to become 'a magnet of Fashion', with the help of sidekicks Puff and Rattle. The book mocks the 'trafficking spirit of the times' that has replaced the stationary gentry values of Mr Oldways. The resort project crumbles and Mr Flimflam goes bankrupt – rather of course like Henry Austen.

But there was an alternative to this backward-looking, nostalgic view. George Crabbe, another of Jane Austen's favourite poets, lived in the ungentrified East Anglian coastal town of Aldeburgh and contemplated:

> . . . these half-buried buildings next the beach;
> Where hang at open doors the net and cork,

While squalid sea-dames mend the meshy work;
Till comes the hour, when, fishing through the tide,
The weary husband throws his freight aside;
A living mass, which now demands the wife,
Th' alternate labours of their humble life.

from 'The Borough'

So, not everyone was antagonistic when, during the second half of the eighteenth century, speculators began transforming – conservatives would say 'deforming' – dowdy fishing hamlets into competing tourist venues, encouraging the invalid and the fun-seeker to throng their beaches and new terraces. With a network of turnpikes (roads with paying points, useful for troop movement in the Napoleonic Wars), travel had become speedier and the middle classes more mobile. The population had burgeoned from five to nine million and by 1800 there were simply more people about with money to spend pursuing entertainment and health.

As the fashion for bathing and drinking sea water took hold, England's south coast bristled with resorts from Teignmouth, Sidmouth, Weymouth and Lyme Regis to Worthing, Brighton, Margate and Ramsgate. Especially welcomed were royal visitors, George III in Weymouth, the Prince Regent in the most famous, Brighton, and ailing Princess Amelia (followed by the Prince Regent's daughter Princess Charlotte) in Worthing. All were greeted enthusiastically with bands and bunting by townspeople who knew the commercial value of a royal body. Poor George III, taking the sea cure following his first bout of maddening porphyria, was faced with a neighbouring bathing machine full of fiddlers who struck up the National Anthem as he emerged from his first plunge.

Yet, even without royal patronage, resorts might do well, although the social level of visitors tended to fall as the century progressed. With their wide seaside walkways for promenading, their terraced lodging houses and seductive shops full of leisure goods, they easily competed with the old inland spas of Bath and Tunbridge Wells for rich invalids, London tourists, fortune hunters and marriageable girls. In *Emma*, Jane Fairfax and her friend both find husbands in Weymouth. The sickly could be blown and drenched into health in the wind and water, while the healthy might enjoy the views or dawdle in the shops and assembly rooms.

Jane at the seaside

The child Jane knew the sea mainly as a place of danger, excitement and derring-do. Her two sailor brothers, Frank and Charles, were at sea most of her adult life, serving on warships and writing home of exotic travels and martial adventures. The heroine of *Persuasion* glories in 'being a sailor's wife' despite 'the tax of quick alarm'.

47

Etching by Thomas Rowlandson from
Poetical Sketches of Scarborough, *1813*

If sailing the seas was men's prerogative, the seaside was wide open to women, and the grown-up Jane loved it. When invited to visit inland, she admitted, 'we greatly prefer the sea to all our relations.'

'All must linger and gaze on a first return to the sea, who ever deserve to look on it at all,' she wrote. She took long exhausting trips to reach the coast whenever she could, and greatly enjoyed bathing and breathing fresh sea air. In *Mansfield Park*, the heroine Fanny Price, miserably exiled in Portsmouth, is yet captivated by 'the ever-varying hues of the sea now at high water, dancing in its glee and dashing against the ramparts with so fine a sound'.

When her family settled in Bath, Jane made the best of the unwelcome change, remarking, 'the prospect of

spending future summers by the Sea or in Wales is very
delightful. – For a time we shall now possess many of the
advantages which I have often thought of with Envy in the
wives of Sailors or Soldiers.' Jane and her family visited
Lyme Regis, Sidmouth, Dawlish, Teignmouth, Worthing
(and elsewhere): they went as far as Wales, to Tenby in the
south and possibly to distant Barmouth far up the west-
ern coast. Despite some inadequate lodgings, Jane seems
readily to have accepted discomfort for the sake of being
by the sea.

On the visit to Lyme in 1804, she wrote, 'The Bathing
was so delightful this morning & Molly so pressing with
me to enjoy myself that I believe I staid in rather too long.'
And again, 'I continue quite well, in proof of which I have
bathed again this morning. It was absolutely necessary
that I should have the little fever and indisposition, which I
had; – it has been all the fashion this week in Lyme.' It was
at Lyme that Cassandra made the famous watercolour portrait of her sister sitting on the grass, bonnet untied: sadly,
a back view.

On the evidence of her letters from Lyme, Jane Austen
went to the sea for pleasure rather than primarily for health:
there's no record of her drinking salt water as a purgative,
even combined with new milk, as some authorities recommended. In her final illness, she turned not to the seaside
for a cure but to inland Cheltenham Spa. If she benefited
from its health-giving waters, however, she did not relish

*Watercolour sketch of Jane Austen
by Cassandra Austen, 1804*

the place in the way she did the seaside resorts – beyond 'the Waters', she found it 'trifling' (Lord Byron disliked even the waters, describing them as 'very medicinal, & sufficiently disgusting'). In a letter to a sick nephew, she wrote, 'Your Physicians I hope will order you to the Sea, or to a house by the side of a very considerable pond.'

The six novels frequently set scenes in resorts, though mostly these remain on the periphery. Each town had a different, sometimes sexy or louche reputation. In the comic tales Jane wrote as a child, fashionable Brighton is one of Lady Lesley's 'favourite haunts of Dissipation'. No wonder Lydia Bennet in *Pride and Prejudice* rushes there to dance and flirt, imagining 'that gay bathing place covered with officers'; from there she runs off with dastardly Wickham. Darcy's sister is almost abducted in Ramsgate, where *Mansfield Park*'s Tom Bertram meets his raffish friends. Frank Churchill enters a clandestine engagement with Jane Fairfax in Weymouth, called by Mr Knightley one of 'the idlest haunts in the kingdom'. By contrast, Anne Elliot recovers her bloom and hopes in slightly more downmarket Lyme.

Although the valetudinarian Mr Woodhouse in *Emma* claims he was nearly killed by the sea, his daughter Isabella is eager to reach muddy Southend to cure 'the weakness in little Bella's throat'. In *Mansfield Park*, Mary Crawford warns Fanny that the sea air may harm her prettiness; in *Sanditon*, while boys run wild, girls must have big bonnets or parasols against sun and wind. Vain Sir Walter Eliot from *Persuasion*, with his horror of the sunburnt, lived-in, masculine face, would have avoided Sanditon: sensibly, when his fecklessness drove him from his ancestral estate, he settled indoors in fading Bath and avoided the sea.

The 'real' Sanditon

Sanditon would have no claim to being a Jane Austen work if fans did not speculate about what town she might have used as model for her invented resort. The distances she mentions and the Parker jaunt to Willingden (said to be on the border of Kent and Sussex) and on to Sanditon, itself a whole mile closer to London than Eastbourne, seem so precise that it is tempting to try to follow the routes on a modern map, factoring in the speed of horses, six to eight miles an hour on indifferent roads. But it won't do. As so often in her novels, Jane Austen has muddied the waters so thoroughly that, beyond the Heywoods' Willingden

Etching by Thomas Rowlandson from
Poetical Sketches of Scarborough, *1813*

being inland somewhere north of Hastings and Eastbourne, nothing certain can be made of the shifty locations: the only secure geographical aspect of Sanditon is that it is not on the map.

Yet, for the model, there are many pretenders. First, Worthing, where Jane Austen stayed for two months in 1805 together with, among others, Cassandra, their mother, Martha Lloyd and Jane's Godmersham friend, Anne Sharp. Worthing was swelling from a small village into a bustling town under the enthusiasm of its developer Edward Ogle. A Mr Ogle was mentioned in a letter to Cassandra, possibly an acquaintance of brother Henry, or just possibly the developer himself or a relative. A speculator in London's docklands as well as Worthing, the energetic Mr Ogle was keen to attract 'select society' to his seaside resort and when eleven-year-old Princess Charlotte, second-in-line to the throne, became a summer tenant of his mansion, Warwick House, he must have thought he'd succeeded. Her visit was celebrated by a dreadful poem which included the lines:

Warwick House is a place I much joy'd at beholding,
Long life to the royal sweet blossom it's holding.

But there are problems with Worthing as the original of Sanditon, the most notable being that it lacks the cliffs that are an essential element of the fictional resort. And some of the description of the much despised Brinshore with its 'putrifying sea weed' and 'insalubrious air' may a little

Worthing, early 1800s

resemble the real early nineteenth-century town which struggled to control invasions of seaweed on its beaches.

Jane Austen visited Lyme Regis in 1803 and 1804, was lyrical about its scenery, and used it as backdrop for some important events in *Persuasion*. One of the early developers of the once small fishing village was Thomas Hollis, who provided the town with its public promenade and lodging houses. The first husband of Lady Denham, Sanditon's patroness, is a Mr Hollis; beyond bequeathing money to his acquisitive spouse, however, Mr Hollis plays no part in the development of Sanditon.

Another claimant is Bognor Regis, founded as a watering-place by a rich shipping merchant and former hatter, Richard Hotham. Flouting humility, he named it Hothampton, which morphed into Bognor. It had a crescent, seafront hotels and in later time a Waterloo Square

(Mr Parker plans a Waterloo Crescent for his Sanditon). Enthusiastic Mr Hotham of Hothampton, much given to puffing his resort, seems to foreshadow Jane Austen's entrepreneur, who boasts:

> My name is Parker, Mr Parker of Sanditon; this lady, my wife Mrs Parker. We are on our road home from London. *My* name perhaps – though I am by no means the first of my family, holding landed property in the parish of Sanditon – may be unknown at this distance from the coast, but Sanditon itself – everybody has heard of Sanditon – the favourite – for a young and rising bathing-place, certainly the favourite spot of all that are to be found along the coast of Sussex – the most favoured by nature, and promising to be the most chosen by man.

As property developer, Mr Hotham was not entirely successful – he saw his resort flooded with French refugees rather than the rich tourists he desired – but he had the advantage of creating his coastal town in the 1790s, in the wartime heyday of the English seaside. After war ended, English resorts like Worthing and Bognor began to lose their shine, as Bath had earlier done – though the nabobs from India or plantation owners from the West Indies, barred from such English delights as long as hostilities continued, would at last be able to visit and flaunt their wealth in a manner Lady Denham, representing older money, much resented. Though notably when she thinks to exploit the fortune of the only West Indian who actually visits Sanditon, the silent Miss Lambe, Lady Denham has no problem with the provenance or use of her money.

When staying at her brother Edward's huge estate of Godmersham in Kent, Jane Austen visited a further claimant, Ramsgate. Brother Frank was posted to Ramsgate in 1803 to raise a corps of 'Sea Fencibles' to defend the Kentish coast: there he met his future wife. In a letter of 1813, Jane made a disparaging remark about the town, noting of an acquaintance that he 'talks of fixing at Ramsgate – Bad Taste!' – though she applauded his desire of settling by the sea. She was given to throwaway comments on places, however, and this one does not disprove the idea that she had Ramsgate (a combined inland farming community and

Hand-painted etching of Ramsgate Harbour c. *1820. Artist unknown.*

coastal fishing hamlet set in a valley between two cliffs) somewhat in mind when she created Sanditon with its cliffs and nearby fishing community. She treated Weymouth in a similar way when she called it 'a shocking place' since ice was unobtainable and the royals departed before they could be ogled. On the East Kent coast, Ramsgate does not work with the cartographical signposts in the novel, but nothing so easy for a writer than to transpose it and its cliffs whole-sale to the south and make it adjacent to the Isle of Wight, which was probably intended to feature in Sidney Parker's truncated story.

As usual when we look for the real-life Pemberley or Mansfield Park or Northanger Abbey, then investigate the various claims, we are brought back to the fact that Jane Austen was a novelist, a creator of fictions and an amal-gamator not a reporter. In the end, no real town, whether it be Worthing, Lyme Regis, Bognor Regis or Ramsgate – or indeed Bexhill or Margate – can be quite like Sanditon and no entrepreneur and speculator as endearingly optimis-tic as Tom Parker.

Jane Austen did not live long enough to witness the rise of Thomas Cook and foreign touring for the middle classes, but, after Waterloo, well-off people could and did travel to the warmer Continent. Indeed, soon after the peace, Henry Austen accompanied two of his richer nephews on a jaunt to Paris, while Jane remarked of a friend that she'd 'frisked off like half England, into Switzerland'. There must always have been some sense of insecurity for the less sanguine landlords of expensive properties and speculators of English seaside resorts.

The shock of Sanditon

Think of the fragment *Sanditon* as a cartoon by James Gillray, Thomas Rowlandson or George Cruikshank. Its characters are based on real people who breathe and walk but in these pages are larger than life, rollickingly exaggerated like caricatures (using the term to mean more than simple crudity). No wonder the younger Austens, grown Victorian in time and old in spirit and years, found it in-

Coloured etching by Thomas Rowlandson, 1815

decorous; it was testament, they thought, to mental as well as physical debility in Aunt Jane.

The Austen family was a large one: Jane's four brothers produced many children and in time she had thirty-three nieces and nephews. Many of these, and their numerous descendants, turned author, and cultivated and fed off the fame of their celebrated relative, so that memories of Austen, completions of her fragments, as well as new works declaring the writers' relationship to Jane Austen, even their ability to 'channel' her, became and continue to be a 'family business'.

Among her nieces and nephews, the most important for her Victorian reputation are the children of James, her eldest brother: James Edward (later Austen-Leigh), his sister Caroline Austen and their half-sister Anna, later Lefroy. After Jane Austen's fame had burgeoned and the last of her generation had died, these three siblings, owning many of the manuscripts, wanted to present their aunt to a respectable late nineteenth-century public. So, they domesticated her image, along with her work.

Using memories from the rest of his family, James Edward Austen-Leigh in 1869 composed a discreet memoir of 'Aunt Jane' and commissioned a prettified engraving to accompany it (using the only known portrait of Jane, a rather acerbic – or perhaps wry – sketch by Cassandra). Needing to touch on some of the unpublished work which he and other family members were known to possess, he tried to avoid jeopardising her increasingly serious reputation by at first hiding those manuscript items which he judged his readership would find unseemly and unladylike. Among these was *Sanditon*. Since there was, however, considerable interest in this final novel, he had to deliver something of it in his second edition: he chose to do so through summary and a few extracts of the comic Parkers. This discretion did not prevent his half-sister Anna Lefroy from beginning, but not concluding, the first of many continuations.

Only in 1925 was Jane Austen's actual text published in full as *Sanditon: Fragment of a Novel*. The subtitle was unprepossessing, unless read in the Romantic context of Keats's and Shelley's inspired poetic fragments. By then Jane Austen was fast becoming one of the pantheon of major

James Edward Austen-Leigh

English novelists, but she had yet to find a place beside the Romantic poets or to be considered within their historical and literary context of transcendental imagination and visionary politics.

James Edward would not have been surprised by some of the negative response: he had anticipated it when forced to produce even the chosen extracts. E. M. Forster, so admiring of the six finished novels, was immune to *Sanditon*'s vitality; he was shocked by its supposed falling-off and saw the effects of 'weakness'. He judged it a sad end to an author who, in her published works, 'never stooped to caricature'. Raised on the notion of the great novelist's ever more subtle psychological realism, even some recent critics condemn the work as the decadence, the annihilation of Jane Austen's great style.

Assuredly *Sanditon* does not take forward the project of recording with verbal minimalism the evanescent inner life of characters for which Austen is famous and for which she was praised by Virginia Woolf among others, nor does it develop her hallmark technique of free indirect speech (when a narrator uses the speech patterns of a character and the two appear merged for a time). But there are other strengths – and of course there are continuities in characters and themes with the six published novels.

Characters like Lady Denham bring echoes of another great lady, Lady Catherine de Bourgh in *Pride and Prejudice*, and Mrs Parker, the pliant wife, useless in a crisis, reminds us of the vegetable Lady Bertram of *Mansfield Park*, unable to do the simplest managerial tasks without her husband. However, unlike Lady Bertram, poor Mrs Parker has an inkling of the foolishness of her spouse and his hypochondriacal sisters, although she lacks the strength to influence them.

There is concern, too, for the vulnerable female predicament, the trials of penniless young women. Clara Brereton reprises the poor and beautiful Jane Fairfax of *Emma*, for example, while the predatory courtship she suffers suggests Fanny Price being pursued by Henry Crawford. But the mood is distinct. Seduction, so dangerous in *Sense and Sensibility* and *Mansfield Park*, becomes comic here: Sir Edward reduces Clara's proposed fate to the 'quietest sort of ruin', while the narrator is clear that the lovely Clara has no intention of being seduced, even quietly. So too with vulnerability. The need for men and the threat of men exist in the shadows. But the Beaufort girls visiting the resort of Sanditon use the concealing blinds in their lodgings to make their displays more appealing, not to hide – and the only named spectator is fat, lethargic Arthur.

Like *Emma*, *Sanditon* delights in capturing fragmented language from disordered minds, but it takes the habit to new heights. The characters rattle on uninterrupted and self-exposing, the relative lack of manuscript reworking suggesting the author wrote most fluently in these monologues. No one is quite 'conversible', to use a resonant Jane

Austen word, no one much communicates with another
though they talk constantly. Miss Bates from *Emma* could
have lived contentedly in Sanditon instead of Highbury:
like the Parkers she needs no interlocutors for her dizzying
displays.

All here must be hyperbolic, words, things and people.
Every summer season must improve on the last: there must
be more houses, more goods, more attractions, more sick
bodies to keep everyone in business and business from
failing – the pattern is 'puffing' or advertising, where
more and more exaggerated claims obscure an underlying
reality. A few people socially below Jane Austen's mainly
middle class and gentry subjects populate all the novels,
but in *Sanditon* far more emerge, usually from the accelerated speech of the principal characters: butlers, gardeners,
maids, a shepherd, old female cottagers, a truculent coachman, Stringer and his son setting up as market gardeners,
Mrs Whitby the librarian and her daughter, William Heeley
the shoemaker, Jebb the milliner, old Sam at the hotel, plus
the 'cooks, housemaids, washerwomen and bathing women'
summoned by Diana Parker for a supposedly helpless Mrs
Griffiths. Bodily symptoms, especially of the Parker siblings, proliferate and grow more outrageous as they are
addressed and narrated.

Jane Austen intended the grotesque, multiplying effects
of *Sanditon*. Revisions to her manuscript frequently exag-
gerate eccentricities and idiosyncrasies of character, making

the exhibition and mathematics of illness more rather than less colourful, for example. In revision, Susan Parker faints not on 'poor Arthur's sneezing' but on 'poor Arthur's trying to suppress a cough'. Diana claims to have rubbed a sprained ankle 'without intermission' for 'six' hours, the 'six' revised upwards from 'four'. The three extracted teeth and the six leeches a day for ten days remain as Austen originally wrote them, absurd and hyperbolic; likewise, the paralysis of a whole right side caused by a cup of green tea, the fasting for a week after a journey, and the multiple insomnia nights of Diana Parker and her curiously resilient invalid sister.

In *Sanditon* the sick often seem more vigorous than the healthy, delighting in their supposed afflictions and the paraphernalia of medicines and remedies as thoroughly as Tom Parker delights in the luxury commodities and visitors. As he enjoys the physical reality of what he has created, so Diana, Susan and Arthur regard with interest and affection their own particular and sympathetic body parts. In addition, Diana is interested in the ailments of others and she desires 'more particulars' of her brother's hurt ankle. She homes in on sickly new arrivals, and timid Miss Lambe will soon be exposed to her vigorous help when they enter a bathing machine together. Invalidism is a career choice and a competitive one, displayed without shame, indeed with pride. Diana advertises the family symptoms with as much gusto as Tom Parker advertises the fine features of his resort.

Etching by Thomas Rowlandson, 1823

Mockery of the health-obsessed runs through Jane Austen's work. Mrs Bennet of *Pride and Prejudice* has some reason to be afflicted by nerves, but she none the less irritates her daughters and amuses the reader with her complaints; Mrs Churchill in *Emma* is regarded as a malingerer until she dies at just the right moment for the happiness of the young lovers. In *Love and Freindship* from her teenage writings, the sentimental heroine gives the physical moral of her decline and impending death:

'One fatal swoon has cost me my Life ... Beware of swoons Dear Laura ... A frenzy fit is not one quarter so pernicious; it is an exercise to the Body and if not too violent, is I dare say conducive to Health in its consequences – Run mad as often as you chuse; but do not faint —'.

These were the last words she ever addressed to me . . . It was her dieing Advice to her afflicted Laura, who has ever most faithfully adhered to it.

Scoffing at medical men, the Parker sisters become self-medicators, concocting their own potions and 'bitters'. Their physical remedies are wonderful, absurd and painful: lengthy friction for a sprain, for example, and teeth-pulling without any anaesthetic.

Their obsessions about diet and allergies do, however, have a modern ring as we ourselves discover more and more possible allergens and require multiple types of tea for a small tea party.

Sanditon is full of muddled minds as well as erratic demanding bodies. The manic mistakes of the obsessive and self-deluded reveal self-ignorance but also show up the inevitable and constant gap between how we think of ourselves and how we appear and sound to others. People misinterpret and misremember in what is almost a beached Ship of Fools. The book opens with Tom Parker taking the wrong road, having misread an advertisement in his impatient zeal to be doing something, no matter what. He believes his 'sad invalid' sisters won't come to Sanditon

'A Calm' by James Gillray, 1810

because of the absence of medical men, when in fact they heartily distrust doctors and are quite capable of rushing round the country on a whim. Sir Edward, patron of the 'circulating library', confuses literary quotations and tumbles over his long, ridiculous words, using them, he hopes, as a form of seduction. Diana Parker gets entangled in her 'wheels within wheels' through her busy-bodying urge to be constantly 'running around' and be in the middle of other people's lives. Indeed, the circle is a good metaphor not only for the trivial existence of restless people, as the narrator remarks, but for the novel itself. The resort depends on the circular repetitive motion of seasons, and visitors must return again and again to make the same learnt remarks about seascapes and weather and descant on the same topics of ailments and prices.

Instead of reason and common sense, characters in Sanditon follow intuition, hunches, 'sensations' and bodily signs. The imagination of Mr Parker is so fertile that he comes to believe that desire can be translated into physical facts and that speech can transform fantasy into reality. But, in the end, not even his transforming will can make a labourers' cottage into a surgeon's picturesque dwelling (*cottages ornés* have to be built *specifically* for tourists, rather like present-day palm-and-bamboo huts by private beaches in tropical sea resorts). Nor can anyone else's imagination quite see a flourishing cliff town for people of 'fortune and fashion' from a few random signs in the lower village: ladies with camp stools in a farm courtyard, a harp above a baker's shop, blue shoes and nankin boots in the cobbler's window, though Tom Parker exclaims 'civilization' at the sight of them. Diana's firm mental convictions cannot separate Mrs Griffths's rich family of invalids from the Camberwell ladies' seminary when the bodies actually stand before her. As so often in *Sanditon*, two things become one; so also the two dead husbands of Lady Denham combine to give her wealth and status. Or one becomes two, as with the originally conflated Willesdens and new and old Sanditons. Nothing in this fragment is quite stable.

For as long as possible, speculation and imagination will push against reality. It's as though there were a mist over people's eyes by the seaside. When Sidney Parker arrives, at first only a child makes him out. There is a whiteness that obscures distinct sight and understanding – the white curtains, the young ladies' incongruous white dresses, and the 'something white and womanish' that 'sober-minded' Charlotte sees through the 'great thickness of air' in Lady Denham's garden on almost the last page of the fragment. Is it simply that Clara's white ribbons give her away, or something more startling?

National tea and toast

*'Have you remembered to collect pieces for the Patchwork?'
(Jane Austen's letter). Square for a Jane Austen commemorative
quilt, sewn by Jane Austen Hampshire Group, 2017*

Sanditon glances wryly at English national self-esteem with its mention of Trafalgar and Waterloo, its touches of wealth and empire. It worries at what seemed so secure in the finished novels. Mr Parker leaves his family estate declaring to his nostalgic wife that, by moving to the top of a windy cliff, they have avoided 'the yearly nuisance of its decaying vegetation'. 'Who can endure a cabbage bed in October?' he asks, though earlier on he had seen the failure to raise its own cabbages as the horror of neighbouring Brinshore. It's hard to imagine Mr Knightley of Donwell Abbey or indeed Mr Darcy of Pemberley turning his back on English agriculture in this way.

The pretty English scene that Emma so much admires within Mr Knightley's ancient Donwell estate, both for itself and for its connection with the past and her family, gives way in *Sanditon* to a sublime 'view' of the mobile sea, to be sold to as many sightseers as possible. In the wartime novels, *Mansfield Park* and *Persuasion*, the sea is still the place of fighting and professional men, of England's naval and imperial prowess, and the coastal towns are full of structures for defence of the land; here in Sanditon, with no fear of French invaders, the seaside exists solely to pleasure the disabled and provide fun and joy for the able.

In popular culture from Los Angeles to Pakistan, Jane Austen is associated with quaint pastoral Englishness. Tea in Austen-themed cafés, accompanied by merchandise of pink patterned teapots and expensively packaged tea leaves, is regarded as quintessentially English, part of a diminished political but saleable cultural identity. In the eighteenth and early nineteenth centuries, however, it seemed a less trivial habit. Tea-drinking was accepted as a national pastime, associated (according to viewpoint) with the civilising or emasculating effect of women. Jonas Hanway took the second view, ranting against it as a risk to the nation and probable ruination of the labouring classes who aped their betters with this effete habit.

Tea-drinking was accompanied by buttered toast. This was the very sign and symbol of English comfort. It required convivial effort and the social informality on which the English prided themselves against formal Continentals. Even Percy Bysshe Shelley, the most ethereal of Romantic poets, wrote, 'let's be merry: we'll have tea and toast.' When he arrived at an English country house, P. G. Wodehouse, creator of Jeeves and Bertie Wooster, rejoiced in 'the cup of tea, the crackling logs and buttered toast; the general atmosphere of leisured cosiness'. For imprisoned Toad in *Wind in the Willows*, buttered toast is the ultimate English comfort food: its smell 'talked of warm kitchens, of breakfasts on bright frosty mornings'. Jane Austen herself is associated with such toast-making. Largely exempted from routine household chores in Chawton by Cassandra and Martha Lloyd, she remained responsible for the tea-caddy and for preparing the breakfast toast.

In Sanditon, instead of hurrying to walk along the cliffs

and breathe salt air like his older brother Tom, lazy young Arthur Parker, all of twenty-one, settles down snugly for toast and (expensive) cocoa with his sickly tea-drinking sisters and the disapproving Charlotte. It's as well no wine is on offer, for Arthur memorably opines that 'the more wine I drink (in moderation) the better I am'. Now, here in lodgings, the fire is lit and the windows closed against the bracing weather as he expresses his bliss in 'relaxation of the languid frame/By soft recumbency of outstretched limbs' as Cowper put it. Then he summons the family energy for toasting. The entrance of the servant with the tea things

> produced a great and immediate change. The young man's attentions were instantly lost. He took his own cocoa from the tray – which seemed provided with almost as many tea-pots &c as there were persons in company, Miss Parker drinking one sort of herb-tea and Miss Diana another – and turning completely to the fire, sat coddling and cooking it to his own satisfaction and toasting some slices of bread, brought up ready-prepared in the toast rack; and, till it was all done, [Charlotte] heard nothing of his voice but the murmuring of a few broken sentences of self-approbation and success.

The tea party is so excessive that it swims out of the novel to become as much of a freak show as the hypochondriacs themselves. Is it a mockery of sentimental English domesticity or a sly celebration?

No answer, for we readers are abandoned soon after. Here and throughout the fragment, we are left with a sense of universal absurdity, a suspicion that all of us live through the imaginary – working on our minds or bodies, detaching desire from common sense. We become uneasy, dis-eased, with bodies supposedly fascinating to others as well as to ourselves, or minds ludicrously ennobled and distorted

'Morning Dress', 1797

by the fantastical world of books. How we, along with the characters, step off the shifting sand of self-obsession and speculation and place our feet back on safe rock is not explained by *Sanditon*, for the brilliant fragment remains enigmatic from beginning to open end.

Sanditon

Chapter 1

A gentleman and lady travelling from Tunbridge towards that part of the Sussex coast which lies between Hastings and Eastbourne, being induced by business to quit the high road, and attempt a very rough lane, were overturned in toiling up its long ascent, half rock, half sand. The accident happened just beyond the only gentleman's house near the lane, a house, which their driver, on being first required to take that direction, had conceived to be necessarily their object, and had with most unwilling looks been constrained to pass by.

He had grumbled and shaken his shoulders so much indeed, and pitied and cut his horses so sharply, that he might have been open to the suspicion of overturning them on purpose (especially as the carriage was not his master's) if the road had not indisputably become considerably worse than before as soon as the premises of the said house were left behind — expressing with a most intelligent portentous countenance that beyond it no wheels but cart wheels could safely proceed.[1]

The severity of the fall was broken by their slow pace and the narrowness of the lane, and, the gentleman having scrambled out and helped out his companion, they neither of them at first felt more than shaken and bruised. But the gentleman had in the course of the extrication sprained his foot, and soon becoming sensible of it was obliged in a few moments to cut short both his remonstrance to the driver and his congratulations to his wife and himself, and sit down on the bank, unable to stand.

'There is something wrong here,' said he, putting his hand to his ankle. 'But never mind, my dear,' looking up at her with a smile, 'it could not have happened, you know, in a better place. — Good out of evil —. The very thing perhaps to be wished for. We shall soon get relief. — *There*, I fancy lies my cure,' pointing to the neat-looking end of a cottage, which was seen romantically situated among wood on a high eminence at some little distance. 'Does not *that* promise to be the very place?'

His wife fervently hoped it was, but stood, terrified and anxious, neither able to do or suggest anything, and receiving her first real comfort from the sight of several persons now coming to their assistance.

The accident had been discerned from a hayfield adjoining the house they had passed, and the persons who approached were a well-looking, hale, gentlemanlike man of middle age, the proprietor of the place, who happened to be among his haymakers at the time, and three or four of the ablest of them summoned to attend their master, to say nothing of all the rest of the field, men, women and children, not very far off.

CHAPTER I

Mr. Heywood, such was the name of the said proprietor, advanced with a very civil salutation — much concern for the accident — some surprise at anybody's attempting that road in a carriage — and ready offers of assistance.

His courtesies were received with good-breeding and gratitude and, while one or two of the men lent their help to the driver in getting the carriage upright again, the traveller said, 'You are extremely obliging Sir, and I take you at your word. The injury to my leg is I dare say very trifling, but it is always best in these cases to have a surgeon's opinion without loss of time; and as the road does not seem at present in a favourable state for my getting up to his house myself, I will thank you to send off one of these good people for the surgeon.'

'The surgeon, Sir!' replied Mr. Heywood. 'I am afraid you will find no surgeon at hand here, but I dare say we shall do very well without him.'

'Nay, Sir, if *he* is not in the way, his partner will do just as well — or rather better. — I would rather see his partner indeed — I would prefer the attendance of his partner. — One of these good people can be with him in three minutes I am sure. I need not ask whether I see the house' (looking towards the cottage), 'for excepting your own, we have passed none in this place which can be the abode of a gentleman.'

Mr. Heywood looked very much astonished and replied,

'What, Sir! are you expecting to find a surgeon in that cottage? We have neither surgeon nor partner in the parish I assure you.'

'Excuse me, Sir,' replied the other. 'I am sorry to have the appearance of contradicting you — but though from the extent of the parish or some other cause you may not be aware of the fact — Stay — can I be mistaken in the place? — Am I not in Willingden? — Is not this Willingden?'

'Yes, Sir, this is certainly Willingden.'

'Then, Sir, I can bring proof of your having a surgeon in the parish, whether you may know it or not. Here, Sir' (taking out his pocket book) 'if you will do me the favour of casting your eye over these advertisements, which I cut out myself from the *Morning Post* and the *Kentish Gazette* only yesterday morning in London, I think you will be convinced that I am not speaking at random. You will find it an advertisement, Sir, of the dissolution of a partnership in the medical line — in your own parish — extensive business — undeniable character — respectable references — wishing to form a separate establishment. — You will find it at full length, Sir,' offering him the two little oblong extracts.

'Sir,' said Mr. Heywood with a good-humoured smile, 'if you were to show me all the newspapers that are printed in one week throughout the kingdom, you would not persuade me of there being a surgeon in Willingden, for, having lived here ever since I was born, man and boy, fifty-seven years, I think I must have *known* of such a person, at least I may venture to say that he has not *much business*. To be sure, if gentlemen were to be often attempting this lane in post-chaises, it might not be a bad speculation for a surgeon to get a house at the top of the hill. But as to that cottage, I can assure you, Sir, that it is in fact (in spite of its spruce air at this distance) as indifferent a double tenement as any in the parish, and that my shepherd lives at one end, and three old women at the other.'

He took the pieces of paper as he spoke and, having looked them over, added, 'I believe I can explain it, Sir. Your mistake is in the place. There are two Willingdens in this county — and your advertisements refer to the other — which is Great Willingden or Willingden Abbots, and lies seven miles off, on the other side of Battle — quite down in the Weald. And *we* Sir' (speaking rather proudly) 'are not in the Weald.'[2]

'Not *down* in the Weald I am sure, Sir,' replied the traveller, pleasantly. 'It took us half an hour to climb your hill. — Well, Sir — I dare say it is as you say, and I have made an abominably stupid blunder. — All done in a moment; — the advertisements did not catch my eye till the last half hour of our being in town — when everything was in the hurry and confusion which always attend a short stay there. — One is never able to complete anything in the way of business you know till the carriage is at the door — and accordingly satisfying myself with a brief enquiry, and finding we were actually to pass within a mile or two of a *Willingden*, I sought no farther . . . My dear,' (to his wife) 'I am very sorry to have brought you into this scrape. But do not be alarmed about my leg. It gives me no pain while I am quiet — and, as soon as these good people have succeeded in setting the carriage to rights and turning the horses round, the best thing we can do will be to measure back our steps into the turnpike road and proceed to Hailsham, and so home, without attempting anything farther. Two hours take us home from Hailsham — and when once at home, we have our remedy at hand you know. — A little of our own bracing sea air will soon set me on my feet again. — Depend upon it, my dear, it is exactly a case for the sea. Saline air and immersion will be the very thing. — My sensations tell me so already.'

In a most friendly manner Mr. Heywood here interposed, entreating them not to think of proceeding till the ankle had been examined, and some refreshment taken, and very cordially pressing them to make use of his house for both purposes.

'We are always well stocked,' said he, 'with all the common remedies for sprains and bruises, and I will answer for the pleasure it will give my wife and daughters to be of service to you and this lady in every way in their power.'

A twinge or two in trying to move his foot disposed the traveller to think rather more as he had done at first of the

benefit of immediate assistance, and, consulting his wife in
the few words of 'Well, my dear, I believe it will be better
for us', turned again to Mr. Heywood and said, 'Before
we accept your hospitality, Sir — and in order to do away
any unfavourable impression which the sort of wild goose-
chase you find me in, may have given rise to — allow me
to tell you who we are. My name is Parker — Mr. Parker
of Sanditon; — this lady, my wife Mrs. Parker. — We
are on our road home from London. — *My* name perhaps — though I am by no means the first of my family
holding landed property in the parish of Sanditon — may
be unknown at this distance from the coast — but Sanditon
itself — everybody has heard of Sanditon, — the favourite — for a young and rising bathing-place, certainly the
favourite spot of all that are to be found along the coast of
Sussex; — the most favoured by Nature, and promising to
be the most chosen by man.'

'Yes, I have heard of Sanditon,' replied Mr. Heywood.
'Every five years, one hears of some new place or other
starting up by the sea, and growing the fashion. How they
can half of them be filled, is the wonder! *Where* people can
be found with money or time to go to them! Bad things for
a country; — sure to raise the price of provisions and make
the poor good for nothing — as I dare say you find, Sir.'[3]

'Not at all, Sir, not at all,' cried Mr. Parker eagerly.
'Quite the contrary I assure you. — A common idea —
but a mistaken one. It may apply to your large, overgrown

places, like Brighton or Worthing or Eastbourne — but *not* to a small village like Sanditon, precluded by its size from experiencing any of the evils of civilization, while the growth of the place, the buildings, the nursery grounds, the demand for everything, and the sure resort of the very best company, those regular, steady, private families of thorough gentility and character who are a blessing everywhere, excite the industry of the poor and diffuse comfort and improvement among them of every sort. — No, Sir, I assure you, Sanditon is not a place . . .'

'I do not mean to take exceptions to *any* place in particular, Sir,' answered Mr. Heywood. 'I only think our coast is too full of them altogether. But had we not better try to get you . . .'

'Our coast too full,' repeated Mr. Parker. 'On that point perhaps we may not totally disagree; — at least there are *enough*. Our coast is abundant enough; it demands no more. — Everybody's taste and everybody's finances may be suited — and those good people who are trying to add to the number are in my opinion excessively absurd, and must soon find themselves the dupes of their own fallacious calculations. Such a place as Sanditon, Sir, I may say was wanted, was called for. — Nature had marked it out — had spoken in most intelligible characters — the finest, purest sea breeze on the coast — acknowledged to be so — excellent bathing — fine hard sand — deep water ten yards from the shore — no mud — no weeds — no slimy rocks — never was there a place more palpably designed by Nature for the resort of the invalid — the very spot which thousands seemed in need of — the most desirable distance from London! One complete, measured mile nearer than Eastbourne. Only conceive, Sir, the advantage of saving a whole mile, in a long journey. But Brinshore, Sir, which I dare say you have in your eye — the attempts of two or three speculating people about Brinshore, this last year, to raise that paltry hamlet, lying as it does between a stagnant marsh, a bleak moor and the constant effluvia of a ridge of putrifying seaweed, can end in nothing but their own disappointment. What in the name of common sense is to *recommend* Brinshore? — A most insalubrious air — roads proverbially detestable — water brackish beyond example, impossible to get a good dish of tea within three miles of the place — and as for the soil — it is so cold and ungrateful that it can hardly be made to yield a cabbage. — Depend upon it, Sir, that this is a faithful description of Brinshore — not in the smallest degree exaggerated — and if you have heard it differently spoken of . . .'

'Sir, I never heard it spoken of in my life before,' said Mr. Heywood. 'I did not know there was such a place in the world.'

'You did not! There, my dear' (turning with exultation to his wife), 'you see how it is. So much for the celebrity of Brinshore! This gentleman did not know there was such a place in the world. Why, in truth, Sir, I fancy we may apply to Brinshore that line of the poet Cowper in his description of the religious cottager, as opposed to Voltaire — "*She*, never heard of half a mile from home".'[4]

'With all my heart, Sir, apply any verses you like to it, but I want to see something applied to your leg, and I am sure by your lady's countenance that she is quite of my opinion and thinks it a pity to lose any more time. — And here come my girls to speak for themselves and their mother' (two or three genteel looking young women, followed by as many maidservants, were now seen issuing from the house) — 'I began to wonder the bustle should not have reached *them*. — A thing of this kind soon makes a stir in a lonely place like ours. — Now, Sir, let us see how you can be best conveyed into the house.'

The young ladies approached and said everything that was proper to recommend their father's offers, and in an unaffected manner calculated to make the strangers easy; and, as Mrs. Parker was exceedingly anxious for relief, and her husband, by this time, not much less disposed for it, a very few civil scruples were enough, especially as the carriage being now set up, was discovered to have received such injury on the fallen side as to be unfit for present use. Mr. Parker was therefore carried into the house, and his carriage wheeled off to a vacant barn.

Chapter 2

The acquaintance, thus oddly begun, was neither short nor unimportant. For a whole fortnight the travellers were fixed at Willingden, Mr. Parker's sprain proving too serious for him to move sooner.

He had fallen into very good hands. The Heywoods were a thoroughly respectable family, and every possible attention was paid in the kindest and most unpretending manner to both husband and wife. *He* was waited on and nursed, and *she* cheered and comforted with unremitting kindness, and as every office of hospitality and friendliness was received as it ought, as there was not more good will on one side than gratitude on the other, nor any deficiency of generally pleasant manners on either, they grew to like each other in the course of that fortnight exceedingly well.

Mr. Parker's character and history were soon unfolded. All that he understood of himself, he readily told, for he was very open-hearted; and, where he might be himself in the dark, his conversation was still giving information to such of the Heywoods as could observe. By such he was perceived to be an enthusiast — on the subject of Sanditon, a complete enthusiast. Sanditon — the success of Sanditon as a small, fashionable bathing place was the object for which he seemed to live. A very few years ago and it had been a quiet village of no pretensions; but some natural advantages in its position and some accidental circumstances having suggested to himself, and the other principal landholder, the probability of its becoming a profitable speculation, they had engaged in it, and planned and built, and praised and puffed, and raised it to a something of young renown — and Mr. Parker could now think of very little besides.

The facts, which in more direct communication he laid before them, were that he was about five and thirty, had been married — very happily married seven years — and had four sweet children at home; that he was of a respectable family, and easy though not large fortune; no profession, succeeding as eldest son to the property which two or three generations had been holding and accumulating before him; that he had two brothers and two sisters — all single and all independent, the eldest of the two former indeed, by collateral inheritance, quite as well provided for as himself.

His object in quitting the high road, to hunt for an advertising surgeon, was also plainly stated; it had not proceeded from any intention of spraining his ankle or doing himself any other injury for the good of such surgeon, nor (as Mr. Heywood had been apt to suppose) from any design of entering into partnership with him; it was merely in consequence of a wish to establish some medical man at Sanditon, which the nature of the advertisement induced him to expect to accomplish in Willingden. He was convinced that the advantage of a medical man at hand would very materially promote the rise and prosperity of the place — would in fact tend to bring a prodigious influx; — nothing else was wanting. He had *strong* reason to believe that *one* family had been deterred last year from trying Sanditon on that account — and probably very many more — and his own sisters, who were sad invalids, and whom he was very anxious to get to Sanditon this summer, could hardly be expected to hazard themselves in a place where they could not have immediate medical advice.

Upon the whole, Mr. Parker was evidently an amiable family-man, fond of wife, children, brothers and sisters, and generally kind-hearted; liberal, gentlemanlike, easy to please; of a sanguine turn of mind, with more imagination than judgement. And Mrs. Parker was as evidently a gentle, amiable, sweet-tempered woman, the properest wife in the world for a man of strong understanding, but not of capacity to supply the cooler reflection which her own husband sometimes needed, and so entirely waiting to be guided on every occasion that, whether he were risking his fortune or spraining his ankle, she remained equally useless.

Sanditon was a second wife and four children to him — hardly less dear — and certainly more engrossing. — He could talk of it for ever. — It had indeed the highest claims; — not only those of birth place, property, and home, — it was his mine, his lottery, his speculation and his hobby horse; his occupation, his hope and his futurity. — He was extremely desirous of drawing his good friends at Willingden thither; and his endeavours in the cause were as grateful and disinterested as they were warm. — He wanted to secure the promise of a visit — to get as many of the family as his own house would contain to follow him to Sanditon as soon as possible — and healthy as they all undeniably were — foresaw that every one of them would be benefited by the sea.

He held it indeed as certain that no person could be really well, no person (however upheld for the present by fortuitous aids of exercise and spirits in a semblance of health) could be really in a state of secure and permanent health without spending at least six weeks by the sea every year. — The sea air and sea bathing together were nearly infallible, one or the other of them being a match for every disorder, of the stomach, the lungs or the blood; they were anti-spasmodic, anti-pulmonary, anti-septic, anti-bilious and anti-rheumatic.[5] Nobody could catch cold by the sea, nobody wanted appetite by the sea, nobody wanted spirits, nobody wanted strength. — They were healing, soft[en]-ing, relaxing — fortifying and bracing — seemingly just as was wanted — sometimes one, sometimes the other. — If the sea breeze failed, the sea-bath was the certain correc-tive; — and, where bathing disagreed, the sea breeze alone was evidently designed by nature for the cure.

His eloquence however could not prevail. Mr. and Mrs. Heywood never left home. Marrying early and having a very numerous family, their movements had been long limited to one small circle; and they were older in habits than in age. Excepting two journeys to London in the year to receive his dividends, Mr. Heywood went no farther than his feet or his well-tried old horse could carry him, and Mrs. Heywood's adventurings were only now and then to visit her neighbours, in the old coach which had been new when they married and fresh lined on their eldest son's coming of age ten years ago.

They had very pretty property — enough, had their family been of reasonable limits, to have allowed them a very gentlemanlike share of luxuries and change, enough for them to have indulged in a new carriage and better roads, an occasional month at Tunbridge Wells, and symptoms of the gout and a winter at Bath; but the maintenance, education and fitting out of fourteen children demanded a very quiet, settled, careful course of life, and obliged them to be stationary and healthy at Willingden. What prudence had at first enjoined was now rendered pleasant by habit. They never left home, and they had a gratification in saying so.

But very far from wishing their children to do the same, they were glad to promote *their* getting out into the world, as much as possible. *They* stayed at home, that their children *might* get out; and while making that home extremely comfortable, welcomed every change from it which could give useful connections or respectable acquaintance to sons or daughters. When Mr. and Mrs. Parker therefore ceased

from soliciting a family visit, and bounded their views to
carrying back one daughter with them, no difficulties were
started. It was general pleasure and consent.

Their invitation was to Miss Charlotte Heywood, a very
pleasing young woman of two and twenty, the eldest of the
daughters at home, and the one who under her mother's
directions had been particularly useful and obliging to
them; who had attended them most, and knew them best.
Charlotte was to go — with excellent health, to bathe and
be better if she could — to receive every possible pleasure
which Sanditon could be made to supply by the gratitude
of those she went with — and to buy new parasols, new
gloves, and new brooches for her sisters and herself at the
library which Mr. Parker was anxiously wishing to support.[6] All that Mr. Heywood himself could be persuaded to
promise was, that he would send everyone to Sanditon who
asked his advice, and that nothing should ever induce him
(as far as the future could be answered for) to spend even
five shillings at Brinshore.

Chapter 3

Every neighbourhood should have a great lady. The great
lady of Sanditon was Lady Denham; and in their journey
from Willingden to the coast Mr. Parker gave Charlotte

a more detailed account of her than had been called for before.

She had been necessarily often mentioned at Willingden for, being his colleague in speculation, Sanditon itself could not be talked of long without the introduction of Lady Denham, and that she was a very rich old lady who had buried two husbands, who knew the value of money, was very much looked up to and had a poor cousin living with her, were facts already well known; but some further particulars of her history and her character served to lighten the tediousness of a long hill, or a heavy bit of road, and to give the visiting young lady a suitable knowledge of the person with whom she might now expect to be daily associating.

Lady Denham had been a rich Miss Brereton, born to wealth but not to education. Her first husband had been a Mr. Hollis, a man of considerable property in the county, of which a large share of the parish of Sanditon, with manor and mansion house, made a part. He had been an elderly man when she married him; her own age about thirty. Her motives for such a match could be little understood at the distance of forty years, but she had so well nursed and pleased Mr. Hollis that at his death he left her everything — all his estates, and all at her disposal.

After a widowhood of some years, she had been induced to marry again. The late Sir Harry Denham, of Denham Park in the neighbourhood of Sanditon, had succeeded in removing her and her large income to his own domains, but he could not succeed in the views of permanently enriching his family which were attributed to him. She had been too wary to put anything out of her own power — and when on Sir Harry's decease she returned again to her own house at Sanditon, she was said to have made this boast to a friend, 'that though she had *got* nothing but her title from the family, still she had *given* nothing for it'. For the title, it was to be supposed that she had married — and Mr. Parker acknowledged there being just such a degree of value for it apparent now, as to give her conduct that natural explanation.

'There is at times,' said he, 'a little self-importance, but it is not offensive; and there are moments, there are points, when her love of money is carried greatly too far. But she is a good-natured woman, a very good-natured woman — a very obliging, friendly neighbour; a cheerful, independent, valuable character — and her faults may be entirely imputed to her want of education. She has good natural sense, but quite uncultivated. She has a fine active mind, as well as a fine healthy frame for a woman of seventy, and enters into the improvement of Sanditon with a spirit truly admirable — though now and then, a littleness *will* appear. She cannot look forward quite as I would have her — and takes alarm at a trifling present expense, without considering what returns it *will* make her in a year or two.

'That is — we think *differently*, we now and then see things *differently*, Miss Heywood. — Those who tell their own story you know must be listened to with caution. — When you see us in contact, you will judge for yourself.'

Lady Denham was indeed a great lady beyond the common wants of society, for she had many thousands a year to bequeath, and three distinct sets of people to be courted by: her own relations, who might very reasonably wish for her original thirty thousand pounds among them; the legal heirs of Mr. Hollis, who must hope to be more indebted to *her* sense of justice than he had allowed them to be to *his*; and those members of the Denham family whom her second husband had hoped to make a good bargain for.[7]

By all of these, or by branches of them, she had no doubt been long, and still continued to be, well attacked; and, of these three divisions, Mr. Parker did not hesitate to say that Mr. Hollis's kindred were the *least* in favour and Sir Harry Denham's the *most*. The former he believed had done themselves irremediable harm by expressions of very unwise and unjustifiable resentment at the time of Mr. Hollis's death; the latter, to the advantage of being the remnant of a connection which she certainly valued, joined those of having been known to her from their childhood and of being always at hand to preserve their interest by reasonable attention.

Sir Edward, the present baronet, nephew to Sir Harry, resided constantly at Denham Park; and Mr. Parker had little doubt that he and his sister Miss Denham, who lived with him, would be principally remembered in her will. He sincerely hoped it. — Miss Denham had a very small provision — and her brother was a poor man for his rank in society.

'He is a warm friend to Sanditon,' said Mr. Parker, 'and his hand would be as liberal as his heart, had he the power. He would be a noble coadjutor! — As it is, he does what he can — and is running up a tasteful little *cottage orné* on a strip of waste ground Lady Denham has granted him — which I have no doubt we shall have many a candidate for, before the end even of *this* season.'[8]

Till within the last twelvemonth, Mr. Parker had considered Sir Edward as standing without a rival, as having the fairest chance of succeeding to the greater part of all that she had to give — but there was now another person's claims to be taken into the account, those of the young female relation whom Lady Denham had been induced to receive into her family. After having always protested against any such addition, and long and often enjoyed the repeated defeats she had given to every attempt of her relations to introduce this young lady or that young lady as a companion at Sanditon House, she had brought back with her from London last Michaelmas a Miss Brereton, who bid fair by her merits to vie in favour with Sir Edward, and to secure for herself and her family that share of the accumulated property which they had certainly the best right to inherit.

Mr. Parker spoke warmly of Clara Brereton, and the interest of his story increased very much with the introduction of such a character. Charlotte listened with more than amusement now; it was solicitude and enjoyment, as she heard her described to be lovely, amiable, gentle, unassuming, conducting herself uniformly with great good sense, and evidently gaining by her innate worth on the affections of her patroness.

Beauty, sweetness, poverty and dependence do not want the imagination of a man to operate upon. With due exceptions, woman feels for woman very promptly and compassionately. He gave the particulars which had led to Clara's admission at Sanditon as no bad exemplification of that mixture of character, that union of littleness with kindness with good sense with even liberality, which he saw in Lady Denham.

After having avoided London for many years, and principally on account of these very cousins who were continually writing, inviting and tormenting her, and whom she was determined to keep at a distance, she had been obliged to go there last Michaelmas with the certainty of being detained at least a fortnight. She had gone to an hotel, living, by her own account, as prudently as possible, to defy the reputed expensiveness of such a home, and at the end of three days calling for her bill, that she might judge of her state.

Its amount was such as determined her on staying not another hour in the house, and she was preparing in all the anger and perturbation which a belief of very gross imposition *there*, and an ignorance of *where* to go for better usage, to leave the hotel at all hazards, when the cousins, the politic and lucky cousins, who seemed always to have a spy on her, introduced themselves at this important moment, and, learning her situation, persuaded her to accept such a home for the rest of her stay as their humbler house in a very inferior part of London could offer.

She went, was delighted with her welcome and the hospitality and attention she received from everybody, found her good cousins the Breretons beyond her expectation worthy people, and finally was impelled, by a personal knowledge of their narrow income and pecuniary difficulties, to invite one of the girls of the family to pass the winter with her.

The invitation was to *one*, for six months, with the probability of another being then to take her place. But, in *selecting* the one, Lady Denham had shown the good part of her character — for passing by the actual *daughters* of the house, she had chosen Clara, a niece — more helpless and more pitiable of course than any — and dependant on poverty — an additional burden on an encumbered circle — and one who had been so low in every worldly view, as with all her natural endowments and powers to have been preparing for a situation little better than a nursery maid.

Clara had returned with her, and by her good sense and merit had now, to all appearance, secured a very strong hold in Lady Denham's regard. The six months had long been over, and not a syllable was breathed of any change or exchange.

She was a general favourite; the influence of her steady conduct and mild, gentle temper was felt by everybody. The prejudices which had met her at first in some quarters were all dissipated. She was felt to be worthy of trust — to be the very companion who would guide and soften Lady Denham — who would enlarge her mind and open her hand. — She was as thoroughly amiable as she was lovely — and since having had the advantage of their Sanditon breezes, that loveliness was complete.

Chapter 4

'And whose very snug-looking place is this?' said Charlotte, as in a sheltered dip within two miles of the sea, they passed close by a moderate-sized house, well fenced and planted, and rich in the garden, orchard and meadows which are the best embellishments of such a dwelling. 'It seems to have as many comforts about it as Willingden.'

'Ah!' said Mr. Parker. 'This is my old house — the house of my forefathers — the house where I and all my brothers and sisters were born and bred — and where my own three eldest children were born — where Mrs. Parker and I lived till within the last two years — till our new house was finished. — I am glad you are pleased with it. — It is an honest old place — and Hillier keeps it in very good order. I have given it up you know to the man who occupies the chief of my land. *He* gets a better house by it — and I, a rather better situation!

'One other hill brings us to Sanditon — modern Sanditon — a beautiful spot. — Our ancestors, you know, always built in a hole. — Here were we, pent down in this little contracted nook, without air or view, only one mile and three quarters from the noblest expanse of ocean between the South Foreland and the Land's End, and without the smallest advantage from it. You will not think I have made a bad exchange when we reach Trafalgar House — which, by the bye, I almost wish I had not named Trafalgar — for Waterloo is more the thing now. [9] However, Waterloo is in reserve — and if we have encouragement enough this year for a little Crescent to be ventured on — (as I trust we shall), then we shall be able to call it Waterloo Crescent — and the name joined to the form of the building, which always takes, will give us the command of lodgers. — In a good season we should have more applications than we could attend to.'

'It was always a very comfortable house,' said Mrs. Parker, looking at it through the back window with something like the fondness of regret. 'And such a nice garden — such an excellent garden.'

'Yes, my love, but *that* we may be said to carry with us. *It* supplies us, as before, with all the fruit and vegetables we want; and we have in fact all the comfort of an excellent kitchen garden, without the constant eyesore of its formalities, or the yearly nuisance of its decaying vegetation. Who can endure a cabbage bed in October?'

'Oh! dear — yes. — We are quite as well off for garden stuff as ever we were — for, if it is forgot to be brought at any time, we can always buy what we want at Sanditon House. — The gardener there is glad enough to supply us. — But it was a nice place for the children to run about in. So shady in summer!'

'My dear, we shall have shade enough on the hill and more than enough in the course of a very few years. The growth of my plantations is a general astonishment. In the mean while we have the canvas awning, which gives us the most complete comfort within doors — and you can get a parasol at Whitby's for little Mary at any time, or a large bonnet at Jebbs'. — And as for the boys, I must say I would rather *them* run about in the sunshine than not. I am sure we agree, my dear, in wishing our boys to be as hardy as possible.'

'Yes indeed, I am sure we do, and I will get Mary a little parasol, which will make her as proud as can be. How grave she will walk about with it, and fancy herself quite a little woman. — Oh! I have not the smallest doubt of our being a great deal better off where we are now. If we any of us

want to bathe, we have not a quarter of a mile to go. —
But you know' (still looking back) 'one loves to look at an
old friend, at a place where one has been happy. — The
Hilliers did not seem to feel the storms last winter at all. —
I remember seeing Mrs. Hillier after one of those dreadful
nights, when *we* had been literally rocked in our bed, and
she did not seem at all aware of the wind being anything
more than common.'

'Yes, yes — that's likely enough. *We* have all the grandeur of the storm, with less real danger, because the wind
meeting with nothing to oppose or confine it around our
house, simply rages and passes on — while down in this
gutter — nothing is known of the state of the air below the
tops of the trees — and the inhabitants may be taken totally
unawares by one of those dreadful currents which should
do more mischief in a valley when they *do* arise than an
open country ever experiences in the heaviest gale.

'But, my dear love — as to garden stuff, — you were
saying that any accidental omission is supplied in a moment
by Lady Denham's gardener — but it occurs to me that we
ought to go elsewhere upon such occasions — and that old
Stringer and his son have a higher claim. I encouraged him
to set up — and am afraid he does not do very well — that
is, there has not been time enough yet. — He *will* do very
well beyond a doubt — but at first it is up hill work; and
therefore we must give him what help we can — and, when
any vegetables or fruit happen to be wanted — and it will

not be amiss to have them often wanted, to have something or other forgotten most days — just to have a nominal supply you know, that poor old Andrew may not lose his daily job — but in fact to buy the chief of our consumption of the Stringers.'

'Very well, my love, that can be easily done — and cook will be satisfied — which will be a great comfort, for she is always complaining of old Andrew now, and says he never brings her what she wants. — There — now the old house is quite left behind. What is it your brother Sidney says about its being a hospital?'

'Oh! my dear Mary, merely a joke of his. He pretends to advise me to make a hospital of it. He pretends to laugh at my improvements. Sidney says anything, you know. He has always said what he chose of and to us all. Most families have such a member among them I believe, Miss Heywood. There is a someone in most families privileged by superior abilities or spirits to say anything. — In ours, it is Sidney, who is a very clever young man, and with great powers of pleasing. — He lives too much in the world to be settled; that is his only fault. — He is here and there and everywhere. I wish we may get him to Sanditon. I should like to have you acquainted with him. — And it would be a fine thing for the place! — Such a young man as Sidney, with his neat equipage and fashionable air. — You and I, Mary, know what effect it might have: many a respectable family, many a careful mother, many a pretty daughter, might it secure us, to the prejudice of Eastbourne and Hastings.'

They were now approaching the church and real village of Sanditon, which stood at the foot of the hill they were afterwards to ascend — a hill whose side was covered with the woods and enclosures of Sanditon House and whose height ended in an open down where the new buildings might soon be looked for. A branch only of the valley, winding more obliquely towards the sea, gave a passage to an inconsiderable stream, and formed at its mouth a third habitable division, in a small cluster of fisherman's houses.

The village contained little more than cottages, but the spirit of the day had been caught, as Mr. Parker observed with delight to Charlotte, and two or three of the best of them were smartened up with a white curtain and 'Lodgings to let', and farther on, in the little green court of an old farm house, two females in elegant white were actually to be seen with their books and camp stools — and in turning the corner of the baker's shop, the sound of a harp might be heard through the upper casement.[10]

Such sights and sounds were highly blissful to Mr. Parker. Not that he had any personal concern in the success of the village itself; for, considering it as too remote from the beach, he had done nothing there — but it was a most valuable proof of the increasing fashion of the place alto-gether. If the *village* could attract, the hill might be nearly full. — He anticipated an amazing season. — At the same time last year (late in July), there had not been a single lodger in the village! — nor did he remember any during the whole summer, excepting one family of children who came from London for sea air after the whooping cough and whose mother would not let them be nearer the shore for fear of their tumbling in.

'Civilization, civilization indeed!' cried Mr. Parker, delighted. 'Look my dear Mary — Look at William Heeley's windows. — Blue shoes, and nankin boots! — Who would have expected such a sight at a shoemaker's in old Sanditon! — This is new within the month. There was no blue shoe when we passed this way a month ago. — Glorious indeed! — Well, I think I *have* done something in my day. Now, for our hill, our health-breathing hill.'

In ascending, they passed the lodge-gates of Sanditon House, and saw the top of the house itself among its groves. It was the last building of former days in that line of the parish. A little higher up, the modern began; and in crossing the down, a Prospect House, a Bellevue Cottage, and a Denham Place were to be looked at by Charlotte with the calmness of amused curiosity, and by Mr. Parker with the eager eye which hoped to see scarcely any empty houses.

More bills at the window than he had calculated on; and a smaller show of company on the hill — fewer carriages, fewer walkers. He had fancied it just the time of day for them to be all returning from their airings to dinner. — But the sands and the terrace always attracted some — and the tide must be flowing — about half-tide now. — He longed to be on the sands, the cliffs, at his own house and everywhere out of his house at once. His spirits rose with the very sight of the sea and he could almost feel his ankle getting stronger already.

Trafalgar House, on the most elevated spot on the down, was a light elegant building, standing in a small lawn with a very young plantation round it, about an hundred yards from the brow of a steep, but not very lofty cliff, and the nearest to it of every building excepting one short row of smart-looking houses called the Terrace with a broad walk in front, aspiring to be the Mall of the place. In this row were the best milliner's shop and the library — a little detached from it, the hotel and billiard room. Here began the descent to the beach, and to the bathing machines, and this was therefore the favourite spot for beauty and fashion.[11]

At Trafalgar House, rising at a little distance behind the Terrace, the travellers were safely set down, and all was happiness and joy between Papa and Mama and their children; while Charlotte, having received possession of her apartment, found amusement enough in standing at her ample, Venetian window, and looking over the miscellaneous foreground of unfinished buildings, waving linen, and tops of houses, to the sea, dancing and sparkling in sunshine and freshness.

Chapter 5

When they met before dinner, Mr. Parker was looking over letters.

'Not a line from Sidney!' said he. 'He is an idle fellow. I sent him an account of my accident from Willingden, and thought he would have vouchsafed me an answer. — But perhaps it implies that he is coming himself. — I trust it may. — But here is a letter from one of my sisters. *They* never fail me. — Women are the only correspondents to be depended on.

'Now Mary' (smiling at his wife), 'before I open it, what shall we guess as to the state of health of those it comes from — or rather what would Sidney say if he were here? — Sidney is a saucy fellow, Miss Heywood. — And you must know, he will have it there is a good deal of imagination in my two sisters' complaints — but it really is not so — or very little. — They have wretched health, as you have heard us say frequently, and are subject to a variety of very serious disorders. — Indeed, I do not believe they know what a day's health is; — and at the same time, they are such excellent, useful women and have so much energy of character that, where any good is to be done, they force themselves on exertions which, to those who do not thoroughly know them, have an extraordinary appearance. — But there is really no affectation about them. They have only weaker constitutions and stronger minds than are often met with, either separate or together. — And our youngest brother, who lives with them, and who is not much above twenty, I am sorry to say, is almost as great an invalid as themselves. — He is so delicate that he can engage in no profession. — Sidney laughs at him — but it really is no joke — though Sidney often makes me laugh at them all in spite of myself. — Now, if he were here, I know he would be offering odds, that either Susan, Diana or Arthur would appear by this letter to have been at the point of death within the last month.'

Having run his eye over the letter, he shook his head and began: 'No chance of seeing them at Sanditon I am sorry to say. — A very indifferent account of them indeed. Seriously, a *very* indifferent account. — Mary, you will be quite sorry to hear how ill they have been and are. — Miss Heywood, if you will give me leave, I will read Diana's letter aloud. — I like to have my friends acquainted with each other — and I am afraid this is the only sort of acquaintance I shall have the means of accomplishing between you. — And I can have no scruple on Diana's account — for her letters show her exactly as she is, the most active, friendly, warm-hearted being in existence, and therefore must give a good impression.'

He read: 'My dear Tom, we were all much grieved at your accident, and if you had not described yourself as fallen into such very good hands, I should have been with you at all hazards the day after the receipt of your letter, though it found me suffering under a more severe attack than usual of my old grievance, spasmodic bile, and hardly able to crawl from my bed to the sofa. — But how were you treated? — Send me more particulars in your next. — If indeed a simple sprain, as you denominate it, nothing would have been so judicious as friction, friction by the hand alone, supposing it could be applied *instantly*.

'Two years ago, I happened to be calling on Mrs. Sheldon when her coachman sprained his foot as he was cleaning the carriage and could hardly limp into the house — but by the immediate use of friction alone, steadily persevered in (and I rubbed his ankle with my own hand for six hours without intermission) — he was well in three days.

'Many thanks, my dear Tom, for the kindness with respect to us, which had so large a share in bringing on your accident. — But pray: never run into peril again in looking for an apothecary on our account, for, had you the most experienced man in his line settled at Sanditon, it would be no recommendation to us. We have entirely done with the whole medical tribe. We have consulted physician after physician in vain, till we are quite convinced that they can do nothing for us and that we must trust to our own knowledge of our own wretched constitutions for any relief. — But if you think it advisable for the interest of the *place*, to get a medical man there, I will undertake the commission with pleasure, and have no doubt of succeeding. — I could soon put the necessary irons in the fire.

'As for getting to Sanditon myself, it is quite an impossibility. I grieve to say that I dare not attempt it, but my feelings tell me too plainly that in my present state the sea air would probably be the death of me. — And neither of my dear companions will leave me, or I would promote their going down to you for a fortnight. But in truth, I doubt whether Susan's nerves would be equal to the effort. She has been suffering much from the headache, and six leeches a day for ten days together relieved her so little that we thought it right to change our measures — and, being convinced on examination that much of the evil lay in her gum, I persuaded her to attack the disorder there. She has accordingly had three teeth drawn, and is decidedly better, but her nerves are a good deal deranged. She can only speak in a whisper — and fainted away twice this morning on poor Arthur's trying to suppress a cough. He, I am happy to say, is tolerably well — though more languid than I like — and I fear for his liver.

'I have heard nothing of Sidney since your being together in town, but conclude his scheme to the Isle of Wight has not taken place, or we should have seen him in his way. — Most sincerely do we wish you a good season at Sanditon, and, though we cannot contribute to your beau monde in person, we are doing our utmost to send you company worth having; and think we may safely reckon on securing you two large families, one a rich West Indian from Surrey, the other a most respectable girls' boarding school, or academy, from Camberwell. — I will not tell you how many people I have employed in the business — wheel within wheel. But success more than repays.[12]

'Yours most affectionately — &c.'

'Well,' said Mr. Parker as he finished, 'though I dare say Sidney might find something extremely entertaining in this letter and make us laugh for half an hour together, I declare *I* by myself can see nothing in it but what is either very pitiable or very creditable. — With all their sufferings, you perceive how much they are occupied in promoting the good of others! — So anxious for Sanditon! Two large families — one, for Prospect House probably, the other, for No. 2 Denham Place — or the end house of the Terrace, — and extra beds at the hotel. — I told you my sisters were excellent women, Miss Heywood.'

'And I am sure they must be very extraordinary ones,' said Charlotte. 'I am astonished at the cheerful style of the letter, considering the state in which both sisters appear to be. Three teeth drawn at once! — frightful! — Your sister Diana seems almost as ill as possible, but those three teeth of your sister Susan's are more distressing than all the rest.'

'Oh! — they are so used to the operation — to every operation — and have such fortitude!'

'Your sisters know what they are about, I dare say, but their measures seem to touch on extremes. I feel that, in any illness, *I* should be so anxious for professional advice, so very little venturesome for myself, or anybody I loved! But then, *we* have been so healthy a family that I can be no judge of what the habit of self-doctoring may do.'

'Why, to own the truth,' said Mrs. Parker, 'I *do* think the Miss Parkers carry it too far sometimes — and so do you, my love, you know. — You often think they would be better if they would leave themselves more alone — and especially Arthur. I know you think it a great pity they should give *him* such a turn for being ill.'

'Well, well, my dear Mary — I grant you, it *is* unfortunate for poor Arthur that at his time of life he should be encouraged to give way to indisposition. It *is* bad; — it *is* bad that he should be fancying himself too sickly for any profession — and sit down at one and twenty, on the interest of his own little fortune, without any idea of attempting to improve it, or of engaging in any occupation that may be of use to himself or others. — But let us talk of pleasanter things. — These two large families are just what we wanted. — But — here is something at hand, pleasanter still — Morgan, with his "Dinner on Table".'

Chapter 6

The party were very soon moving after dinner. Mr. Parker could not be satisfied without an early visit to the library, and the library subscription book, and Charlotte was glad to see as much, and as quickly as possible, where all was new.

They were out in the very quietest part of a watering-place day, when the important business of dinner or of sitting after dinner was going on in almost every inhabited lodging. Here and there a solitary elderly man might be seen who was forced to move early and walk for health, but, in general, it was a thorough pause of company. It was emptiness and tranquillity on the Terrace, the cliffs, and the sands. The shops were deserted, the straw hats and pendant lace seemed left to their fate both within the house and without, and Mrs. Whitby at the library was sitting in her inner room reading one of her own novels, for want of employment.

The list of subscribers was but commonplace. The Lady Denham, Miss Brereton, Mr. and Mrs. Parker, Sir Edward Denham and Miss Denham, whose names might be said to lead off the season, were followed by nothing better than — Mrs. Mathews, Miss Mathews, Miss E. Mathews, Miss H. Mathews. — Dr. and Mrs. Brown. — Mr. Richard Pratt. — Lieutenant Smith R. N., Captain Little, Limehouse. — Mrs.

Jane Fisher. Miss Fisher. Miss Scroggs. — Rev. Mr. Hankins. Mr. Beard, solicitor, Gray's Inn. — Mrs. Davis. And Miss Merryweather.

Mr. Parker could not but feel that the list was not only without distinction, but less numerous than he had hoped. It was but July, however, and August and September were the months; — and, besides, the promised large families from Surrey and Camberwell were an ever-ready consolation.

Mrs. Whitby came forward without delay from her literary recess, delighted to see Mr. Parker again, whose manners recommended him to everybody, and they were fully occupied in their various civilities and communications, while Charlotte, having added her name to the list as the first offering to the success of the season, was busy in some immediate purchases for the further good of everybody, as soon as Miss Whitby could be hurried down from her toilette, with all her glossy curls and smart trinkets, to wait on her.

The library, of course, afforded everything: all the useless things in the world that could not be done without, and among so many pretty temptations, and with so much good will for Mr. Parker to encourage expenditure, Charlotte began to feel that she must check herself — or rather she reflected that at two and twenty there could be no excuse for her doing otherwise — and that it would not do for her to be spending all her money the very first evening. She took up a book; it happened to be a volume of *Camilla*. She had not Camilla's youth, and had no intention of having her distress, so she turned from the drawers of rings and brooches, repressed farther solicitation and paid for what she bought.[13]

For her particular gratification, they were then to take a turn on the cliff, but as they quitted the library they were met by two ladies whose arrival made an alteration necessary, Lady Denham and Miss Brereton. They had been to Trafalgar House, and been directed thence to the library, and, though Lady Denham was a great deal too active to regard the walk of a mile as anything requiring rest, and talked of going home again directly, the Parkers knew that to be pressed into their house and obliged to take her tea with them would suit her best, and therefore the stroll on the cliff gave way to an immediate return home.

'No, no,' said Her Ladyship, 'I will not have you hurry your tea on my account. — I know you like your tea late. — My early hours are not to put my neighbours to inconvenience. No, no, Miss Clara and I will get back to our own tea. — We came out with no other thought. — We wanted just to see you and make sure of your being really come — , but we get back to our own tea.'

She went on however towards Trafalgar House and took possession of the drawing room very quietly, without seeming to hear a word of Mrs. Parker's orders to the servant as they entered, to bring tea directly.

Charlotte was fully consoled for the loss of her walk by

finding herself in company with those whom the conversation of the morning had given her a great curiosity to see. She observed them well. Lady Denham was of middle height, stout, upright and alert in her motions with a shrewd eye and self-satisfied air — but not an unagreeable countenance — and though her manner was rather downright and abrupt, as of a person who valued herself on being free-spoken, there was a good humour and cordiality about her — a civility and readiness to be acquainted with Charlotte herself, and a heartiness of welcome towards her old friends, which was inspiring the good will she seemed to feel.

And as for Miss Brereton, her appearance so completely justified Mr. Parker's praise that Charlotte thought she had never beheld a more lovely or more interesting young woman. Elegantly tall, regularly handsome, with great delicacy of complexion and soft blue eyes, a sweetly modest and yet naturally graceful address, Charlotte could see in her only the most perfect representation of whatever heroine might be most beautiful and bewitching in all the numerous volumes they had left behind them on Mrs. Whitby's shelves. Perhaps it might be partly owing to her having just issued from a circulating library, but she could not separate the idea of a complete heroine from Clara Brereton. Her situation with Lady Denham so very much in favour of it! — She seemed placed with her on purpose to be ill-used. — Such poverty and dependence, joined to such beauty and merit, seemed to leave no choice in the business.

These feelings were not the result of any spirit of romance in Charlotte herself. No, she was a very sober-minded young lady, sufficiently well-read in novels to supply her imagination with amusements, but not at all unreasonably influenced by them; and while she pleased herself the first five minutes with fancying the persecutions which *ought* to be the lot of the interesting Clara, especially in the form of the most barbarous conduct on Lady Denham's side, she found no reluctance to admit, from subsequent observation, that they appeared to be on very comfortable terms. She could see nothing worse in Lady Denham than the sort of old-fashioned formality of always calling her *Miss Clara*, nor anything objectionable in the degree of observance and attention which Clara paid. On one side it seemed protecting kindness, on the other grateful and affectionate respect.

The conversation turned entirely upon Sanditon, its present number of visitants and the chances of a good season. It was evident that Lady Denham had more anxiety, more fears of loss, than her coadjutor. She wanted to have the place fill faster, and seemed to have many harassing apprehensions of the lodgings being in some instances underlet. Miss Diana Parker's two large families were not forgotten.

'Very good, very good,' said Her Ladyship. 'A West Indy family and a school. That sounds well. That will bring money.'

'No people spend more freely, I believe, than West Indians,' observed Mr. Parker.

'Aye, so I have heard, and because they have full purses, fancy themselves equal, may be, to your old county families. But then, they who scatter their money so freely, never think of whether they may not be doing mischief by raising the price of things — and I have heard that's very much the case with your West-ingines — and if they come among us to raise the price of our necessaries of life, we shall not much thank them, Mr. Parker.'

'My dear Madam, they can only raise the price of consumable articles by such an extraordinary demand for them and such a diffusion of money among us as must do us more good than harm. — Our butchers and bakers and traders in general cannot get rich without bringing prosperity to *us*. — If *they* do not gain, our rents must be insecure — and in proportion to their profit must be ours eventually in the increased value of our houses.'

'Oh! well. But I should not like to have butcher's meat raised, though — and I shall keep it down as long as I can. Aye — that young lady smiles I see; — I dare say she thinks me an odd sort of a creature, — but *she* will come to care about such matters herself in time. Yes, yes, my dear, depend upon it, you will be thinking of the price of butcher's meat in time — though you may not happen to have quite such a servants' hall to feed as I have. — And I do believe *those* are best off that have fewest servants. — I am not a woman of parade, as all the world knows, and, if it was not for what I owe to poor Mr. Hollis's memory, I should never keep up Sanditon House as I do — it is not for my own pleasure.

'Well, Mr. Parker, and the other is a boarding school, a French boarding school, is it? — No harm in that. — They'll stay their six weeks. — And out of such a number, who knows but some may be consumptive and want asses' milk — and I have two milch asses at this present time. — [14] But perhaps the little Misses may hurt the furniture. — I hope they will have a good sharp governess to look after them.'

Poor Mr. Parker got no more credit from Lady Denham than he had from his sisters for the object which had taken him to Willingden.

'Lord! my dear Sir,' she cried, 'how could you think of such a thing? I am very sorry you met with your accident, but upon my word you deserved it. — Going after a doctor! — Why, what should we do with a doctor here? It would be only encouraging our servants and the poor to fancy themselves ill if there was a doctor at hand. — Oh! pray, let us have none of the tribe at Sanditon. We go on very well as we are. There is the sea and the Downs and my milch-asses — and I have told Mrs. Whitby that if any-body enquires for a chamber horse, they may be supplied at a fair rate — (poor Mr. Hollis's chamber horse, as good as new) — and what can people want for more? — Here have I lived seventy good years in the world and never took physic above twice — and never saw the face of a doctor in all my life on my *own* account. — And I verily believe if my poor dear Sir Harry had never seen one neither, he would have been alive now. — Ten fees, one after another, did the man take who sent *him* out of the world. — I beseech you, Mr. Parker, no doctors here.'

The tea things were brought in.

'Oh! my dear Mrs. Parker — you should not indeed — why would you do so? I was just upon the point of wishing you good evening. But, since you are so very neighbourly, I believe Miss Clara and I must stay.'

Chapter 7

The popularity of the Parkers brought them some visitors the very next morning, amongst them Sir Edward Denham and his sister, who having been at Sanditon House drove on to pay their compliments; and the duty of letter-writing being accomplished, Charlotte was settled with Mrs. Parker in the drawing room in time to see them all.

The Denhams were the only ones to excite particular attention. Charlotte was glad to complete her knowledge of the family by an introduction to them, and found them, the better half at least (for, while single, the *gentleman* may sometimes be thought the better half of the pair) not unworthy notice. Miss Denham was a fine young woman, but cold and reserved, giving the idea of one who felt her consequence with pride and her poverty with discontent, and who was immediately gnawed by the want of a handsomer equipage than the simple gig in which they travelled, and which their groom was leading about still in her sight.[15]

Sir Edward was much her superior in air and manner; certainly handsome, but yet more to be remarked for his very good address and wish of paying attention and giving pleasure. He came into the room remarkably well, talked much — and very much to Charlotte, by whom he chanced to be placed — and she soon perceived that he had a fine countenance, a most pleasing gentleness of voice, and a great deal of conversation. She liked him. — Sober-minded as she was, she thought him agreeable, and did not quarrel with the suspicion of his finding her equally so, which *would* arise, from his evidently disregarding his sister's motion to go, and persisting in his station and his discourse. — I make no apologies for my heroine's vanity. — If there are young ladies in the world at her time of life, more dull of fancy and more careless of pleasing, I know them not, and never wish to know them.

At last, from the low French windows of the drawing room which commanded the road and all the paths across the Down, Charlotte and Sir Edward, as they sat, could not but observe Lady Denham and Miss Brereton walking by; and there was instantly a slight change in Sir Edward's countenance, with an anxious glance after them as they proceeded, followed by an early proposal to his sister not merely for moving, but for walking on together to the Terrace, which altogether gave a hasty turn to Charlotte's fancy, cured her of her half-hour's fever, and placed her in a more capable state of judging, when Sir Edward was gone, of *how* agreeable he had actually been. 'Perhaps there was a good deal in his air and address; and his title did him no harm.'

She was very soon in his company again. The first object of the Parkers, when their house was cleared of morning visitors, was to get out themselves. The Terrace was the attraction to all: everybody who walked must begin with the Terrace, and there, seated on one of the two green benches by the gravel walk, they found the united Denham party. But though united in the gross, very distinctly divided again — the two superior ladies being at one end of the bench, and Sir Edward and Miss Brereton at the other.

Charlotte's first glance told her that Sir Edward's air was that of a lover. — There could be no doubt of his devotion to Clara. — How Clara received it was less obvious — but she was inclined to think not very favourably; for though sitting thus apart with him (which probably she might not have been able to prevent) her air was calm and grave. — That the young lady at the other end of the bench was doing penance was indubitable. The difference in Miss Denham's

CHAPTER 7

countenance, the change from Miss Denham sitting in cold grandeur in Mrs. Parker's drawing-room, to be kept from silence by the efforts of others, to Miss Denham at Lady Denham's elbow, listening and talking with smiling attention or solicitous eagerness, was very striking — and very amusing — or very melancholy, just as satire or morality might prevail. Miss Denham's character was pretty well decided with Charlotte.

Sir Edward's required longer observation. He surprised her by quitting Clara immediately on their all joining and agreeing to walk, and by addressing his attentions entirely to herself. Stationing himself close by her, he seemed to mean to detach her as much as possible from the rest of the party and to give her the whole of his conversation.

He began, in a tone of great taste and feeling, to talk of the sea and the sea shore — and ran with energy through all the usual phrases employed in praise of their sublimity, and descriptive of the *undescribable* emotions they excite in the mind of sensibility. — The terrific grandeur of the ocean in a storm, its glassy surface in a calm, its gulls and its samphire, and the deep fathoms of its abysses, its quick vicissitudes, its direful deceptions, its mariners tempting it in sunshine and overwhelmed by the sudden tempest, all were eagerly and fluently touched; — rather commonplace perhaps — but doing very well from the lips of a handsome Sir Edward, — and she could not but think him a man of feeling — till he began to stagger her by the number of his quotations, and the bewilderment of some of his sentences.

'Do you remember,' said he, 'Scott's beautiful lines on the sea? — Oh! what a description they convey! — They are never out of my thoughts when I walk here. — That man who can read them unmoved must have the nerves of an assassin! — Heaven defend me from meeting such a man unarmed.'

'What description do you mean?' said Charlotte. 'I remember none, at this moment, of the sea in either of Scott's poems.'

'Do not you indeed? — Nor can I exactly recall the beginning at this moment. — But — you cannot have forgotten his description of woman:

"Oh! Woman in our hours of ease" —

Delicious! Delicious! — Had he written nothing more, he would have been immortal. And then again, that unequalled, unrivalled address to parental affection:

"Some feelings are to mortals given
 With less of earth in them than heaven" &c.

'But while we are on the subject of poetry, what think you, Miss Heywood, of Burns's lines to his Mary? — Oh! there is pathos to madden one! — If ever there was a man who *felt*, it was Burns. — Montgomery has all the fire of poetry, Wordsworth has the true soul of it — Campbell in his pleasures of hope has touched the extreme of our sensations:

"Like angel's visits, few and far between." Can you conceive anything more subduing, more melting, more fraught with the deep sublime than that line? — But Burns — I confess my sense of his pre-eminence, Miss Heywood. — If Scott *has* a fault, it is the want of passion. — Tender, elegant, descriptive — but *tame*. — The man who cannot do justice to the attributes of woman is my contempt. — Sometimes indeed a flash of feeling seems to irradiate him — as in the lines we were speaking of — "Oh! Woman in our hours of ease" —. But Burns is always on fire. — His soul was the altar in which lovely woman sat enshrined, his spirit truly breathed the immortal incense which is her due.'[16]

'I have read several of Burns's poems with great delight,' said Charlotte as soon as she had time to speak, 'but I am not poetic enough to separate a man's poetry entirely from his character; and poor Burns's known irregularities greatly interrupt my enjoyment of his lines. I have difficulty in depending on the *truth* of his feelings as a lover. I have not faith in the *sincerity* of the affections of a man of his description. He felt and he wrote and he forgot.'

'Oh! no no,' exclaimed Sir Edward in an ecstasy. 'He was all ardour and truth! — His genius and his susceptibilities might lead him into some aberrations. — But who is perfect? — It were hyper-criticism, it were pseudo-philosophy to expect from the soul of high-toned genius the grovellings of a common mind. — The coruscations of talent, elicited by impassioned feeling in the breast of man, are perhaps

incompatible with some of the prosaic decencies of life; —
nor can you, loveliest Miss Heywood' — (speaking with
an air of deep sentiment) — 'nor can any woman be a fair
judge of what a man may be propelled to say, write or do,
by the sovereign impulses of illimitable ardour.'

This was very fine; but, if Charlotte understood it at all,
not very moral, and, being moreover by no means pleased
with his extraordinary style of compliment, she gravely
answered, 'I really know nothing of the matter. — This is a
charming day. The wind I fancy must be southerly.'

'Happy, happy wind, to engage Miss Heywood's
thoughts!'

She began to think him downright silly. His choosing to
walk with her, she had learnt to understand. It was done to
pique Miss Brereton. She had read it in an anxious glance
or two on his side — but why he should talk so much
nonsense, unless he could do no better, was unintelligible.
He seemed very sentimental, very full of some feelings or
other, and very much addicted to all the newest-fashioned
hard words — had not a very clear brain she presumed,
and talked a good deal by rote. The future might explain
him further — but when there was a proposition for going
into the library she felt that she had had quite enough of Sir
Edward for one morning, and very gladly accepted Lady
Denham's invitation of remaining on the Terrace with her.

The others all left them, Sir Edward with looks of very
gallant despair in tearing himself away, and they united their

agreeableness: that is, Lady Denham, like a true great lady, talked and talked only of her own concerns, and Charlotte listened — amused in considering the contrast between her two companions. Certainly, there was no strain of doubtful sentiment, nor any phrase of difficult interpretation, in Lady Denham's discourse.

Taking hold of Charlotte's arm with the ease of one who felt that any notice from her was an honour, and, communicative from the influence of the same conscious importance or a natural love of talking, she immediately said in a tone of great satisfaction — and with a look of arch sagacity, 'Miss Esther wants me to invite her and her brother to spend a week with me at Sanditon House, as I did last summer. — But I shan't. — She has been trying to get round me every way, with her praise of this, and her praise of that; but I saw what she was about. — I saw through it all. — I am not very easily taken in my dear.'

Charlotte could think of nothing more harmless to be said than the simple enquiry of — 'Sir Edward and Miss Denham?'

'Yes, my dear. *My young folks*, as I call them sometimes, for I take them very much by the hand. I had them with me last summer about this time, for a week; from Monday to Monday; and very delighted and thankful they were. — For they are very good young people, my dear. I would not have you think that I *only* notice them for poor dear Sir Harry's sake. No, no; they are very deserving themselves,

or, trust me, they would not be so much in *my* company. —
I am not the woman to help anybody blindfold. — I always
take care to know what I am about and who I have to deal
with, before I stir a finger. — I do not think I was ever
over-reached in my life; and that is a good deal for a woman
to say that has been married twice.

'Poor dear Sir Harry (between ourselves) thought at first
to have got more. — But' (with a bit of a sigh) 'he is gone,
and we must not find fault with the dead. Nobody could live
happier together than us — and he was a very honourable
man, quite the gentleman of ancient family. — And when
he died, I gave Sir Edward his gold watch.'

She said this with a look at her companion which implied
its right to produce a great impression, and, seeing no rap-
turous astonishment in Charlotte's countenance, added
quickly, 'He did not bequeath it to his nephew, my dear —
it was no bequest. It was not in the will. He only told me,
and *that* but once, that he should wish his nephew to have
his watch; but it need not have been binding, if I had not
chosen it.'

'Very kind indeed! very handsome!' said Charlotte,
absolutely forced to affect admiration.

'Yes, my dear — and it is not the *only* kind thing I have
done by him. — I have been a very liberal friend to Sir
Edward. And poor young man, he needs it bad enough; —
for, though I am *only* the *dowager*, my dear, and he is
the *heir*, things do not stand between us in the way they

commonly do between those two parties. — Not a shilling do I receive from the Denham estate. Sir Edward has no payments to make *me*. He don't stand uppermost, believe me. — It is *I* that help *him*.'

'Indeed! He is a very fine young man; particularly elegant in his address.'

This was said chiefly for the sake of saying something, but Charlotte directly saw that it was laying her open to suspicion by Lady Denham's giving a shrewd glance at her and replying, 'Yes, yes, he is very well to look at — and it is to be hoped some lady of large fortune will think so — for Sir Edward *must* marry for money. — He and I often talk that matter over. — A handsome young fellow like him will go smirking and smiling about and paying girls compliments, but he knows he *must* marry for money. — And Sir Edward is a very steady young man in the main, and has got very good notions.'

'Sir Edward Denham,' said Charlotte, 'with such personal advantages may be almost sure of getting a woman of fortune, if he chooses it.'

This glorious sentiment seemed quite to remove suspicion.

'Aye my dear — that's very sensibly said,' cried Lady Denham. 'And if we could but get a young heiress to Sanditon! But heiresses are monstrous scarce! I do not think we have had an heiress here, or even a co, since Sanditon has been a public place. Families come after families, but as far as I can learn, it is not one in a hundred of them that have any real property, landed or funded. — An income perhaps, but no property. Clergymen may be, or lawyers from town, or half-pay officers, or widows with only a jointure.[17] And what good can such people do anybody? — except just as they take our empty houses — and (between ourselves) I think they are great fools for not staying at home. Now, if we could get a young heiress to be sent here for her health — (and if she was ordered to drink asses' milk I could supply her) — and as soon as she got well, have her fall in love with Sir Edward!'

'That would be very fortunate indeed.'

'And Miss Esther must marry somebody of fortune too — she must get a rich husband. Ah! young ladies that have no money are very much to be pitied! — But —' after a short pause — 'if Miss Esther thinks to talk me into inviting them to come and stay at Sanditon House, she will find herself mistaken. — Matters are altered with me since last summer you know. — I have Miss Clara with me now, which makes a great difference.'

She spoke this so seriously that Charlotte instantly saw in it the evidence of real penetration and prepared for some fuller remarks, but it was followed only by — 'I have no fancy for having my house as full as an hotel. I should not choose to have my two housemaids' time taken up all the morning, in dusting out bedrooms. — They have Miss Clara's room to put to rights as well as my own every day. — If they had hard places, they would want higher wages.'

For objections of this nature, Charlotte was not prepared, and she found it so impossible even to affect sympathy that she could say nothing.

Lady Denham soon added, with great glee, 'And besides all this, my dear, am I to be filling my house to the prejudice of Sanditon? — If people want to be by the sea, why don't they take lodgings? — Here are a great many empty houses — three on this very terrace; no fewer than three lodging papers staring us in the face at this very moment, Numbers 3, 4 and 8. 8, the corner house, may be too large for them, but either of the two others are nice little snug houses, very fit for a young gentleman and his sister. — And so, my dear, the next time Miss Esther begins talking about the dampness of Denham Park, and the good bathing always does her, I shall advise them to come and take one of these lodgings for a fortnight. — Don't you think that will be very fair? — Charity begins at home you know.'

Charlotte's feelings were divided between amusement and indignation, but indignation had the larger and the increasing share. She kept her countenance and she kept a civil silence. She could not carry her forbearance farther; but without attempting to listen longer, and only conscious that Lady Denham was still talking on in the same way, allowed her thoughts to form themselves into such a meditation as this:

JANE AUSTEN'S SANDITON

'She is thoroughly mean. I had not expected anything so bad. — Mr. Parker spoke too mildly of her. — His judgement is evidently not to be trusted. — His own good nature misleads him. He is too kind-hearted to see clearly. — I must judge for myself. — And their very *connection* prejudices him. — He has persuaded her to engage in the same speculation — and because their object in that line is the same, he fancies she feels like him in others. — But she is very, very mean. — I can see no good in her. — Poor Miss Brereton! — And she makes everybody mean about her. — This poor Sir Edward and his sister, — how far nature meant them to be respectable I cannot tell, — but they are *obliged* to be mean in their servility to her. And I am mean, too, in giving her my attention, with the appearance of coinciding with her. Thus it is, when rich people are sordid.'

Chapter 8

The two ladies continued walking together till rejoined by the others, who as they issued from the library were followed by a young Whitby running off with five volumes under his arm to Sir Edward's gig.

And Sir Edward, approaching Charlotte, said, 'You may perceive what has been our occupation. My sister wanted my counsel in the selection of some books. We have many leisure hours, and read a great deal. I am no indiscriminate novel-reader. The mere trash of the common circulating library, I hold in the highest contempt.[18] You will never hear me advocating those puerile emanations which detail nothing but discordant principles incapable of amalgamation, or those vapid tissues of ordinary occurrences from which no useful deductions can be drawn. — In vain may we put them into a literary alembic; — we distil nothing which can add to science. — You understand me I am sure?'

'I am not quite certain that I do. But if you will describe the sort of novels which you *do* approve, I dare say it will give me a clearer idea.'

'Most willingly, fair questioner. The novels which I approve are such as display human nature with grandeur — such as show her in the sublimities of intense feeling — such as exhibit the progress of strong passion from the first germ of incipient susceptibility to the utmost energies of reason half-dethroned — where we see the strong spark of woman's captivations elicit such fire in the soul of man as leads him — (though at the risk of some aberration from the strict line of primitive obligations) — to hazard all, dare all, achieve all, to obtain her. — Such are the works which I peruse with delight, and I hope I may say, with amelioration. They hold forth the most splendid portraitures of high conceptions, unbounded views, illimitable ardour, indomitable decision, and even when the event is mainly anti-prosperous to the high-toned machinations of the prime character, the potent, pervading hero of the story, it leaves us full of generous emotions for him; — our hearts are paralysed. — 'Twere pseudo-philosophy to assert that we do not feel more enwrapped by the brilliancy of his career than by the tranquil and morbid virtues of any opposing character. Our approbation of the latter is but eleemosynary. — These are the novels which enlarge the primitive capabilities of the heart, and which it cannot impugn the sense, or be any dereliction of the character, of the most anti-puerile man, to be conversant with.'

'If I understand you aright,' said Charlotte, 'our taste in novels is not at all the same.'

And here they were obliged to part, Miss Denham being too much tired of them all to stay any longer.

The truth was that Sir Edward, whom circumstances had confined very much to one spot, had read more sentimental novels than agreed with him. His fancy had been early caught by all the impassioned and most exceptionable parts of Richardson's. And such authors as have since appeared to tread in Richardson's steps, so far as man's determined pursuit of woman in defiance of every opposition of feeling and convenience is concerned, had since occupied the greater part of his literary hours, and formed his character. With a perversity of judgement, which must be attributed to his not having by nature a very strong head, the graces, the spirit, the ingenuity, and the perseverance of the villain of the story outweighed all his absurdities and all his atrocities with Sir Edward. With him, such conduct was genius, fire and feeling. — It interested and inflamed him; and he was always more anxious for its success and mourned over its discomfitures with more tenderness than could ever have been contemplated by the authors.

Though he owed many of his ideas to this sort of reading, it were unjust to say that he read nothing else, or that his language were not formed on a more general knowledge of modern literature. He read all the essays, letters, tours and criticisms of the day — and with the same ill-luck which made him derive only false principles from lessons of morality, and incentives to vice from the history of its overthrow, he gathered only hard words and involved sentences from the style of our most approved writers.

Sir Edward's great object in life was to be seductive. With such personal advantages as he knew himself to possess, and such talents as he did also give himself credit for, he regarded it as his duty. — He felt that he was formed to be a dangerous man — quite in the line of the Lovelaces. — The very name of Sir Edward, he thought, carried some degree of fascination with it.

To be generally gallant and assiduous about the fair, to make fine speeches to every pretty girl, was but the inferior part of the character he had to play. Miss Heywood, or any other young woman with any pretensions to beauty, he was entitled (according to his own views of society) to approach with high compliment and rhapsody on the slightest acquaintance; but it was Clara alone on whom he had serious designs; it was Clara whom he meant to seduce. Her seduction was quite determined on. Her situation in every way called for it. She was his rival in Lady Denham's favour, she was young, lovely and dependant. — He had very early seen the necessity of the case, and had now been long trying with cautious assiduity to make an impression on her heart, and to undermine her principles.

Clara saw through him, and had not the least intention of being seduced, but she bore with him patiently enough to confirm the sort of attachment which her personal charms had raised.

A greater degree of discouragement indeed would not have affected Sir Edward. He was armed against the highest pitch of disdain or aversion. If she could not be won by affection, he must carry her off. He knew his business. Already had he had many musings on the subject. If he *were* constrained so to act, he must naturally wish to strike out something new, to exceed those who had gone before him — and he felt a strong curiosity to ascertain whether the neighbourhood of Timbuctoo might not afford some solitary house adapted for Clara's reception; — but the expense alas! of measures in that masterly style was ill-suited to his purse, and prudence obliged him to prefer the quietest sort of ruin and disgrace for the object of his affections, to the more renowned.

Chapter 9

One day, soon after Charlotte's arrival at Sanditon, she had the pleasure of seeing, just as she ascended from the sands to the Terrace, a gentleman's carriage with post-horses standing at the door of the hotel, as very lately arrived, and by the quantity of luggage taking off, bringing, it might be hoped, some respectable family determined on a long residence.

Delighted to have such good news for Mr. and Mrs. Parker, who had both gone home some time before, she proceeded for Trafalgar House with as much alacrity as could remain after having been contending for the last two hours with a very fine wind blowing directly on shore. But she had not reached the little lawn when she saw a lady walking nimbly behind her at no great distance; and, convinced that it could be no acquaintance of her own, she resolved to hurry on and get into the house if possible before her. But the stranger's pace did not allow this to be accomplished; Charlotte was on the steps and had rung, but the door was not opened when the other crossed the lawn; and, when the servant appeared, they were just equally ready for entering the house.

The ease of the lady, her 'How do you do Morgan?' and Morgan's looks on seeing her, were a moment's astonishment, but another moment brought Mr. Parker into the hall to welcome the sister he had seen from the drawing room, and she was soon introduced to Miss Diana Parker.

There was a great deal of surprise but still more pleasure in seeing her. Nothing could be kinder than her reception from both husband and wife. 'How did she come? and with whom? — And they were so glad to find her equal to the journey! — And that she was to belong to *them*, was a thing of course.'

Miss Diana Parker was about four and thirty, of middling height and slender, delicate looking rather than sickly, with an agreeable face and a very animated eye; her manners resembling her brother's in their ease and frankness, though with more decision and less mildness in her tone. She began an account of herself without delay — thanking them for their invitation, but '*that* was quite out of the question, for they were all three come, and meant to get into lodgings and make some stay.'

'All three come! — What! — Susan and Arthur! — Susan able to come too! — This was better and better.'

'Yes — we are actually all come. Quite unavoidable. — Nothing else to be done. — You shall hear all about it. — But my dear Mary, send for the children; — I long to see them.'

'And how has Susan borne the journey? — and how is Arthur? — and why do not we see him here with you?'

'Susan has borne it wonderfully. She had not a wink

of sleep either the night before we set out, or last night at Chichester, and, as this is not so common with her as with *me*, I have had a thousand fears for her — but she has kept up wonderfully — had no hysterics of consequence till we came within sight of poor old Sanditon — and the attack was not very violent — nearly over by the time we reached your hotel — so that we got her out of the carriage extremely well, with only Mr. Woodcock's assistance — and when I left her she was directing the disposal of the luggage and helping old Sam uncord the trunks. — She desired her best love, with a thousand regrets at being so poor a creature that she could not come with me. And as for poor Arthur, he would not have been unwilling himself, but there is so much wind that I did not think he could safely venture — for I am *sure* there is lumbago hanging about him — and so I helped him on with his great coat and sent him off to the Terrace, to take us lodgings. — Miss Heywood must have seen our carriage standing at the hotel. — I knew Miss Heywood the moment I saw her before me on the Down. — My dear Tom I am glad to see you walk so well. Let me feel your ankle. — That's right; all right and clean. The play of your sinews a *very* little affected — barely perceptible. — Well — now for the explanation of my being here. — I told you in my letter, of the two considerable families I was hoping to secure for you — the West Indians, and the seminary.'

Here Mr. Parker drew his chair still nearer to his sister, and took her hand again most affectionately as he answered,

'Yes, yes; — how active and how kind you have been!'

'The West Indians,' she continued, 'whom I look upon as the *most* desirable of the two — as the best of the good — prove to be a Mrs. Griffiths and her family. I know them only through others. — You must have heard me mention Miss Capper, the particular friend of *my* very particular friend Fanny Noyce; — now, Miss Capper is extremely intimate with a Mrs. Darling, who is on terms of constant correspondence with Mrs. Griffiths herself. — Only a *short* chain, you see, between us, and not a link wanting. Mrs. Griffiths meant to go to the sea for her young people's benefit — had fixed on the coast of Sussex, but was undecided as to the where, wanted something private, and wrote to ask the opinion of her friend Mrs. Darling. — Miss Capper happened to be staying with Mrs. Darling when Mrs. Griffiths's letter arrived, and was consulted on the question; *she* wrote the same day to Fanny Noyce and mentioned it to her — and Fanny, all alive for *us*, instantly took up her pen and forwarded the circumstance to me — except as to *names* — which have but lately transpired. — There was but *one* thing for *me* to do. — I answered Fanny's letter by the same post and pressed for the recommendation of Sanditon. Fanny had feared your having no house large enough to receive such a family. — But I seem to be spinning out my story to an endless length. — You see how it was all managed. I had the pleasure of hearing soon afterwards by the same simple link of connection that Sanditon *had been* recommended by Mrs. Darling, and that the West Indians were very much disposed to go thither. — This was the state of the case when I wrote to you; — but two days ago — yes, the day before yesterday — I heard again from Fanny Noyce, saying that *she* had heard from Miss Capper, who by a letter from Mrs. Darling understood that Mrs. Griffiths has expressed herself in a letter to Mrs. Darling more doubtingly on the subject of Sanditon. — Am I clear? — I would be anything rather than not clear.'

'Oh! perfectly, perfectly. Well?'

'The reason of this hesitation, was her having no connections in the place, and no means of ascertaining that she should have good accommodations on arriving there; — and she was particularly careful and scrupulous on all those matters more on account of a certain Miss Lambe, a young lady (probably a niece) under her care, than on her own account or her daughters'. — Miss Lambe has an immense fortune — richer than all the rest — and very delicate health. — One sees clearly enough by all this, the *sort* of woman Mrs. Griffiths must be — as helpless and indolent as wealth and a hot climate are apt to make us. But we are not all born to equal energy. — What was to be done? I had a few moments' indecision — whether to offer to write to *you* or to Mrs. Whitby to secure them a house? — but neither pleased me. — I hate to employ others, when I am equal to act myself — and my conscience told me that this was an occasion which called for me. Here was a family of helpless invalids whom I might essentially serve. — I sounded Susan — the same thought had occurred to her. — Arthur made no difficulties — our plan was arranged immediately, we were off yesterday morning at six — , left Chichester at the same hour today — and here we are.'

'Excellent! Excellent!' cried Mr. Parker. 'Diana, you are unequalled in serving your friends and doing good to all the world. — I know nobody like you. — Mary, my love, is not she a wonderful creature? — Well — and now, what house do you design to engage for them? — What is the size of their family?'

'I do not at all know,' replied his sister, 'have not the least idea — never heard any particulars; — but I am very sure that the largest house at Sanditon cannot be *too* large. They are more likely to want a second. — I shall take only one, however, and that but for a week certain. — Miss Heywood, I astonish you. — You hardly know what to make of me. — I see by your looks, that you are not used to such quick measures.'

The words 'Unaccountable officiousness! — Activity run mad!' had just passed through Charlotte's mind, but a civil answer was easy. 'I dare say I do look surprised,' said she, 'because these are very great exertions, and I know what invalids both you and your sister are.'

'Invalids indeed. — I trust there are not three people in England who have so sad a right to that appellation. — But, my dear Miss Heywood, we are sent into this world to be as extensively useful as possible, and, where some degree of strength of mind is given, it is not a feeble body which will excuse us — or incline us to excuse ourselves. — The world is pretty much divided between the weak of mind and the strong — between those who can act and those who cannot — and it is the bounden duty of the capable to let no opportunity of being useful escape them. — My sister's complaints and mine are happily not often of a nature to threaten existence *immediately* — and as long as we *can* exert ourselves to be of use to others, I am convinced that the body is the better for the refreshment the mind receives in doing its duty. — While I have been travelling, with this object in view, I have been perfectly well.'

The entrance of the children ended this little panegyric on her own disposition, and, after having noticed and caressed them all, she prepared to go.

'Cannot you dine with us? — Is not it possible to prevail on you to dine with us?' was then the cry; and *that* being absolutely negatived, it was 'And when shall we see you again? and how can we be of use to you?' And Mr. Parker warmly offered his assistance in taking the house for Mrs. Griffiths. 'I will come to you the moment I have dined,' said he, 'and we will go about together.'

But this was immediately declined. 'No, my dear Tom, upon no account in the world shall you stir a step on any business of mine. — Your ankle wants rest. I see by the position of your foot that you have used it too much already. — No, I shall go about my house-taking directly. Our dinner is not ordered till six — and by that time I hope to have completed it. It is now only half past four. — As to seeing *me* again today — I cannot answer for it; the others will be at the hotel all the evening, and delighted to see you at any time, but as soon as I get back I shall hear what Arthur has done about our own lodgings, and probably the moment dinner is over shall be out again on business relative to them, for we hope to get into some lodgings or other and be settled after breakfast tomorrow. — I have not much confidence in poor Arthur's skill for lodging-taking, but he seemed to like the commission.'

'I think you are doing too much,' said Mr. Parker. 'You will knock yourself up. You should not move again after dinner.'

'No, indeed you should not,' cried his wife, 'for dinner is such a mere *name* with you all, that it can do you no good. I know what your appetites are.'

'My appetite is very much mended I assure you lately. I have been taking some bitters of my own decocting, which have done wonders. Susan never eats — I grant you — and just at present *I* shall want nothing; I never eat for about a week after a journey — but as for Arthur, he is only too much disposed for food. We are often obliged to check him.'

'But you have not told me anything of the *other* family coming to Sanditon,' said Mr. Parker as he walked with her to the door of the house, 'the Camberwell seminary; have we a good chance of *them*?'

'Oh! certain — quite certain. — I had forgotten them for the moment, but I had a letter three days ago from my friend Mrs. Charles Dupuis which assured me of Camberwell. Camberwell will be here to a certainty, and very soon. — *That* good woman (I do not know her name) not being so wealthy and independent as Mrs. Griffiths — can travel and choose for herself. — I will tell you how I got at *her*. Mrs. Charles Dupuis lives almost next door to a lady who has a relation lately settled at Clapham, who actually attends the seminary and gives lessons on eloquence and belles lettres to some of the girls. — I got that man a hare from one of Sidney's friends — and he recommended Sanditon — without *my* appearing however — Mrs. Charles Dupuis managed it all.'

Chapter 10

It was not a week since Miss Diana Parker had been told by her feelings that the sea air would probably in her present state be the death of her, and now she was at Sanditon, intending to make some stay, and without appearing to have the slightest recollection of having written or felt any such thing. It was impossible for Charlotte not to suspect a good deal of fancy in such an extraordinary state of health. Disorders and recoveries so very much out of the common way seemed more like the amusement of eager minds in want of employment than of actual afflictions and relief.

The Parkers were no doubt a family of imagination and quick feelings, and, while the eldest brother found vent for his superfluity of sensation as a projector, the sisters were perhaps driven to dissipate theirs in the invention of odd complaints. The *whole* of their mental vivacity was evidently not so employed; part was laid out in a zeal for being useful. It should seem that they must either be very busy for the good of others, or else extremely ill themselves.

Some natural delicacy of constitution in fact, with an unfortunate turn for medicine, especially quack medicine, had given them an early tendency, at various times, to various disorders; the rest of their suffering was from fancy, the love of distinction and the love of the wonderful. They had charitable hearts and many amiable feelings, but a spirit of restless activity, and the glory of doing more than anybody else, had their share in every exertion of benevolence, and there was vanity in all they did, as well as in all they endured.

Mr. and Mrs. Parker spent a great part of the evening at the hotel; but Charlotte had only two or three views of Miss Diana posting over the Down after a house for this lady whom she had never seen, and who had never employed her. She was not made acquainted with the others till the following day, when, being removed into lodgings and all the party continuing quite well, their brother and sister and herself were entreated to drink tea with them.

They were in one of the Terrace houses, and she found them arranged for the evening in a small neat drawing room, with a beautiful view of the sea if they had chosen it, but, though it had been a very fair English summer day, not only was there no open window, but the sofa and the table and the establishment in general was all at the other end of the room by a brisk fire.

Miss Parker, whom, remembering the three teeth drawn in one day, Charlotte approached with a peculiar degree of respectful compassion, was not very unlike her sister in person or manner, though more thin and worn by illness and medicine, more relaxed in air, and more subdued in voice. She talked, however, the whole evening, as incessantly as Diana — and excepting that she sat with salts in her hand, took drops two or three times from one out of the several phials already at home on the mantelpiece, and made a great many odd faces and contortions, Charlotte could perceive no symptoms of illness which she, in the boldness of her own good health, would not have undertaken to cure by putting out the fire, opening the window, and disposing of the drops and the salts by means of one or the other.

She had had considerable curiosity to see Mr. Arthur Parker; and, having fancied him a very puny, delicate-looking young man, the smallest very materially of not a robust family, was astonished to find him quite as tall as his brother and a great deal stouter, broad made and lusty, and with no other look of an invalid than a sodden complexion.

Diana was evidently the chief of the family; principal mover and actor. She had been on her feet the whole morning, on Mrs. Griffiths's business or their own, and was still the most alert of the three. Susan had only superintended their final removal from the hotel, bringing two heavy boxes herself, and Arthur had found the air so cold that he had merely walked from one house to the other as nimbly as he could, and boasted much of sitting by the fire till he had cooked up a very good one.

Diana, whose exercise had been too domestic to admit of calculation, but who, by her own account, had not once sat down during the space of seven hours, confessed herself a little tired. She had been too successful however for much fatigue; for not only had she by walking and talking down a thousand difficulties at last secured a proper house at eight guineas per week for Mrs. Griffiths, she had also opened so many treaties with cooks, housemaids, washerwomen and bathing women that Mrs. Griffiths would have little more to do on her arrival than to wave her hand and collect them around her for choice. Her concluding effort in the cause had been a few polite lines of information to Mrs. Griffiths herself, time not allowing for the circuitous train of intelligence which had been hitherto kept up, and she was now

CHAPTER 10

regaling in the delight of opening the first trenches of an
acquaintance with such a powerful discharge of unexpected
obligation.

Mr. and Mrs. Parker and Charlotte had seen two post-
chaises crossing the Down to the hotel as they were setting
off — a joyful sight — and full of speculation. The Miss
Parkers and Arthur had also seen something; they could
distinguish from their window that there *was* an arrival at
the hotel, but not its amount.

Their visitors answered for two hack-chaises — could it
be the Camberwell seminary?

No — No. Had there been a third carriage, perhaps it
might; but it was very generally agreed that two hack-
chaises could never contain a seminary. Mr. Parker was
confident of another new family.

When they were all finally seated, after some removals
to look at the sea and the hotel, Charlotte's place was by
Arthur, who was sitting next to the fire with a degree of
enjoyment which gave a good deal of merit to his civility
in wishing her to take his chair. There was nothing dubi-
ous in her manner of declining it, and he sat down again
with much satisfaction. She drew back her chair to have
all the advantage of his person as a screen, and was very
thankful for every inch of back and shoulders beyond her
pre-conceived idea.

Arthur was heavy in eye as well as figure, but by no means
indisposed to talk; and, while the other four were chiefly

engaged together, he evidently felt it no penance to have a fine young woman next to him, requiring in common politeness some attention, as his brother, who felt the decided want of some motive for action, some powerful object of animation for him, observed with considerable pleasure.

Such was the influence of youth and bloom that he began even to make a sort of apology for having a fire.

'We should not have one at home,' said he, 'but the sea air is always damp. I am not afraid of anything so much as damp.'

'I am so fortunate,' said Charlotte, 'as never to know whether the air is damp or dry. It has always some property that is wholesome and invigorating to me.'

'*I* like the air too, as well as anybody can,' replied Arthur. 'I am very fond of standing at an open window when there is no wind, — but unluckily a damp air does not like *me*. — It gives me the rheumatism. — You are not rheumatic I suppose?'

'Not at all.'

'That's a great blessing. — But perhaps you are nervous.'

'No, I believe not. I have no idea that I am.'

'*I* am very nervous. — To say the truth — nerves are the worst part of my complaints in *my* opinion. My sisters think me bilious, but I doubt it.'

'You are quite in the right, to doubt it as long as you possibly can, I am sure.'

'If I were bilious,' he continued, 'you know wine would

150

disagree with me, but it always does me good. — The more wine I drink (in moderation) the better I am. — I am always best of an evening. — If you had seen me today before dinner, you would have thought me a very poor creature.'

Charlotte could believe it. She kept her countenance however, and said, 'As far as I can understand what nervous complaints are, I have a great idea of the efficacy of air and exercise for them — daily, regular exercise — and I should recommend rather more of it to *you* than I suspect you are in the habit of taking.'

'Oh! I am very fond of exercise myself,' he replied, 'and mean to walk a great deal while I am here, if the weather is temperate. I shall be out every morning before breakfast — and take several turns upon the Terrace, and you will often see me at Trafalgar House.'

'But you do not call a walk to Trafalgar House much exercise?'

'Not as to mere distance, but the hill is so steep! — Walking up that hill, in the middle of the day, would throw me into such a perspiration! — You would see me all in a bath, by the time I got there! — I am very subject to perspiration, and there cannot be a surer sign of nervousness.'

They were now advancing so deep in physics[19] that Charlotte viewed the entrance of the servant with the tea things as a very fortunate interruption.

It produced a great and immediate change. The young man's attentions were instantly lost. He took his own cocoa from the tray — which seemed provided with almost as many tea-pots &c as there were persons in company, Miss Parker drinking one sort of herb-tea and Miss Diana another — and turning completely to the fire, sat coddling and cooking it to his own satisfaction and toasting some slices of bread, brought up ready-prepared in the toast rack; and, till it was all done, she heard nothing of his voice but the murmuring of a few broken sentences of self-approbation and success.

When his toils were over, however, he moved back his chair into as gallant a line as ever, and proved that he had not been working only for himself by his earnest invitation to her to take both cocoa and toast.

She was already helped to tea, which surprised him, so totally self-engrossed had he been.

'I thought I should have been in time,' said he, 'but cocoa takes a great deal of boiling.'

'I am much obliged to you,' replied Charlotte, 'but I *prefer* tea.'

'Then I will help myself,' said he. 'A large dish of rather weak cocoa every evening agrees with me better than anything.'

It struck her however, as he poured out this rather weak cocoa, that it came forth in a very fine, dark coloured stream — and at the same moment, his sisters both crying out, 'Oh! Arthur, you get your cocoa stronger and stronger every evening—', with Arthur's somewhat conscious

reply of ''*Tis* rather stronger than it should be tonight —'
convinced her that Arthur was by no means so fond of being
starved as they could desire, or as he felt proper himself. He
was certainly very happy to turn the conversation on dry
toast, and hear no more of his sisters.

'I hope you will eat some of this toast,' said he, 'I reckon
myself a very good toaster; I never burn my toasts — I
never put them too near the fire at first — and yet, you see,
there is not a corner but what is well browned. — I hope
you like dry toast.'

'With a reasonable quantity of butter spread over it, very
much,' said Charlotte, 'but not otherwise.'

'No more do I,' said he, exceedingly pleased. 'We think
quite alike there. — So far from dry toast being wholesome,
I think it a very bad thing for the stomach. Without a little
butter to soften it, it hurts the coats of the stomach. I am
sure it does. — I will have the pleasure of spreading some
for you directly, — and afterwards I will spread some for
myself. — Very bad indeed for the coats of the stomach —
but there is no convincing *some* people. — It irritates and
acts like a nutmeg grater.'

He could not get the command of the butter, however,
without a struggle, his sisters accusing him of eating a great
deal too much, and declaring he was not to be trusted; and
he maintaining that he only ate enough to secure the coats
of his stomach; and, besides, he only wanted it now for Miss
Heywood.

Such a plea must prevail; he got the butter and spread away for her with an accuracy of judgement which at least delighted himself; but, when her toast was done, and he took his own in hand, Charlotte could hardly contain herself as she saw him watching his sisters while he scrupulously scraped off almost as much butter as he put on, and then seize an odd moment for adding a great dab just before it went into his mouth.

Certainly, Mr. Arthur Parker's enjoyments in invalidism were very different from his sisters' — by no means so spiritualized. A good deal of earthy dross hung about him. Charlotte could not but suspect him of adopting that line of life principally for the indulgence of an indolent temper, and to be determined on having no disorders but such as called for warm rooms and good nourishment.

In one particular, however, she soon found that he had caught something from *them*. 'What!' said he. 'Do you venture upon two dishes of strong green tea in one evening? — What nerves you must have! — How I envy you. — Now, if *I* were to swallow only one such dish — what do you think its effect would be upon me?'

'Keep you awake perhaps all night,' replied Charlotte, meaning to overthrow his attempts at surprise by the grandeur of her own conceptions.

'Oh! if that were all!' he exclaimed. 'No — it would act on me like poison and entirely take away the use of my right side before I had swallowed it five minutes. — It sounds almost incredible — but it has happened to me so often that I cannot doubt it. — The use of my right side is entirely taken away for several hours!'

'It sounds rather odd to be sure,' answered Charlotte coolly, 'but I dare say it would be proved to be the simplest thing in the world by those who have studied right sides and green tea scientifically and thoroughly understand all the possibilities of their action on each other.'

Soon after tea, a letter was brought to Miss Diana Parker from the hotel.

'From Mrs. Charles Dupuis,' said she, 'some private hand.' And having read a few lines, [she] exclaimed aloud, 'Well, this is very extraordinary! very extraordinary indeed! — That both should have the same name — Two Mrs. Griffiths! — This is a letter of recommendation and introduction to me of the lady from Camberwell — and *her* name happens to be Griffiths too.'

A few lines more however, and the colour rushed into her cheeks, and with much perturbation she added, 'The oddest thing that ever was! — a Miss Lambe too! — a young West Indian of large fortune. — But it *cannot* be the same — impossible that it should be the same.'

She read the letter aloud for comfort. It was merely to 'introduce the bearer, Mrs. Griffiths from Camberwell, and the three young ladies under her care, to Miss Diana Parker's notice. Mrs. Griffiths, being a stranger at Sanditon, was anxious for a respectable introduction, and Mrs.

Charles Dupuis, therefore, at the instance of the interme-
diate friend, provided her with this letter, knowing that
she could not do her dear Diana a greater kindness than by
giving her the means of being useful. Mrs. Griffiths's chief
solicitude would be for the accommodation and comfort of
one of the young ladies under her care, a Miss Lambe, a
young West Indian of large fortune, in delicate health.'

'It was very strange! — very remarkable! — very
extraordinary,' but they were all agreed in determining it
to be *impossible* that there should not be two families; such
a totally distinct set of people as were concerned in the
reports of each made that matter quite certain. There *must*
be two families — impossible to be otherwise. 'Impossible'
and 'Impossible' was repeated over and over again with
great fervour. — An accidental resemblance of names and
circumstances, however striking at first, involved nothing
really incredible — and so it was settled.

Miss Diana herself derived an immediate advantage to
counterbalance her perplexity. She must put her shawl over
her shoulders and be running about again. Tired as she was,
she must instantly repair to the hotel to investigate the truth
and offer her services.

Chapter 11

It would not do. Not all that the whole Parker race could say among themselves could produce a happier catastrophe than that the family from Surrey and the family from Camberwell were one and the same. The rich West Indians, and the young ladies' seminary had all entered Sanditon in those two hack chaises. The Mrs. Griffiths who, in her friend Mrs. Darling's hands, had wavered as to coming and been unequal to the journey, was the very same Mrs. Griffiths whose plans were at the same period (under another representation) perfectly decided, and who was without fears or difficulties.

All that had the appearance of incongruity in the reports of the two might very fairly be placed to the account of the vanity, the ignorance, or the blunders of the many engaged in the cause by the vigilance and caution of Miss Diana Parker. *Her* intimate friends must be officious like herself, and the subject had supplied letters and extracts and messages enough to make everything appear what it was not.

Miss Diana probably felt a little awkward on being first obliged to admit her mistake. A long journey from Hampshire taken for nothing — a brother disappointed — an expensive house on her hands for a week — must have been some of her immediate reflections. And much worse than all the rest must have been the sort of sensation of being less clear-sighted and infallible than she had believed herself. No part of it, however, seemed to trouble her long. There were so many to share in the shame and the blame that probably, when she had divided out their proper portions to Mrs. Darling, Miss Capper, Fanny Noyce, Mrs. Charles Dupuis and Mrs. Charles Dupuis's neighbour, there might be a mere trifle of reproach remaining for herself. At any rate, she was seen all the following morning walking about after lodgings with Mrs. Griffiths, as alert as ever.

Mrs. Griffiths was a very well-behaved, genteel kind of woman, who supported herself by receiving such great girls and young ladies as wanted either masters for finishing their education, or a home for beginning their displays.[20] She had several more under her care than the three who were now come to Sanditon, but the others all happened to be absent.

Of these three, and indeed of all, Miss Lambe was beyond comparison the most important and precious, as she paid in proportion to her fortune. She was about seventeen, half mulatto, chilly and tender, had a maid of her own, was to have the best room in the lodgings, and was always of the first consequence in every plan of Mrs. Griffiths.

The other girls, two Miss Beauforts, were just such young ladies as may be met with in at least one family out of three throughout the kingdom; they had tolerable complexions, showy figures, an upright decided carriage and an assured look; they were very accomplished and very ignorant, their time being divided between such pursuits as might attract admiration and those labours and expedients of dexterous ingenuity by which they could dress in a style much beyond what they *ought* to have afforded; they were some of the first in every change of fashion — and the object of all was to captivate some man of much better fortune than their own.

Mrs. Griffiths had preferred a small, retired place like Sanditon on Miss Lambe's account, and the Miss Beauforts, though naturally preferring anything to smallness and retirement, yet, having in the course of the spring been involved in the inevitable expense of six new dresses each for a three days' visit, were constrained to be satisfied with Sanditon also, till their circumstances were retrieved. There, with the hire of a harp for one, and the purchase of some drawing paper for the other, and all the finery they could already command, they meant to be very economical, very elegant and very secluded; with the hope, on Miss Beaufort's side, of praise and celebrity from all who walked within the sound of her instrument, and on Miss Letitia's, of curiosity and rapture in all who came near her while she sketched — and to both, the consolation of meaning to be the most stylish girls in the place.

The particular introduction of Mrs. Griffiths to Miss Diana Parker secured them immediately an acquaintance with the Trafalgar House family and with the Denhams; and the Miss Beauforts were soon satisfied with 'the circle in which they moved in Sanditon' to use a proper phrase, for everybody must now 'move in a circle' — to the prevalence of which rotatory motion is perhaps to be attributed the giddiness and false steps of many.

Lady Denham had other motives for calling on Mrs. Griffiths besides attention to the Parkers. In Miss Lambe, here was the very young lady, sickly and rich, whom she had been asking for; and she made the acquaintance for Sir Edward's sake, and the sake of her milch asses. How it might answer with regard to the baronet remained to be proved, but, as to the animals, she soon found that all her calculations of profit would be vain. Mrs. Griffiths would not allow Miss Lambe to have the smallest symptom of a decline, or any complaint which asses' milk could possibly relieve. 'Miss Lambe was under the constant care of an experienced physician; and his prescriptions must be their rule', and except in favour of some tonic pills, which a cousin of her own had a property in, Mrs. Griffiths did never deviate from the strict medicinal page.

The corner house of the Terrace was the one in which Miss Diana Parker had the pleasure of settling her new friends, and considering that it commanded in front the favourite lounge of all the visitors at Sanditon, and on one side, whatever might be going on at the hotel, there could not have been a more favourable spot for the seclusions of the Miss Beauforts. And accordingly, long before they had suited themselves with an instrument or with drawing paper, they had, by the frequency of their appearance at the low windows upstairs, in order to close the blinds, or open the blinds, to arrange a flower pot on the balcony, or look at nothing through a telescope, attracted many an eye upwards, and made many a gazer gaze again.

A little novelty has a great effect in so small a place; the Miss Beauforts, who would have been nothing at Brighton, could not move here without notice; and even Mr. Arthur Parker, though little disposed for supernumerary exertion, always quitted the Terrace in his way to his brother's by this corner house, for the sake of a glimpse of the Miss Beauforts — though it was half a quarter of a mile round about and added two steps to the ascent of the hill.

Chapter 12

Charlotte had been ten days at Sanditon without seeing Sanditon House, every attempt at calling on Lady Denham having been defeated by meeting with her beforehand. But now it was to be more resolutely undertaken, at a more early hour, that nothing might be neglected of attention to Lady Denham or amusement to Charlotte.

'And if you should find a favourable opening my love,' said Mr. Parker, who did not mean to go with them, 'I think you had better mention the poor Mullins's situation, and sound Her Ladyship as to a subscription for them. I am not fond of charitable subscriptions in a place of this kind — it is a sort of tax upon all that come — yet as their distress is very great and I almost promised the poor woman yesterday to get something done for her, I believe we must set a subscription on foot, and therefore the sooner the better; and Lady Denham's name at the head of the list will be a very necessary beginning. — You will not dislike speaking to her about it, Mary?'

'I will do whatever you wish me,' replied his wife, 'but you would do it so much better yourself. I shall not know what to say.'

'My dear Mary,' cried he, 'it is impossible you can be really at a loss. Nothing can be more simple. You have only to state the present afflicted situation of the family, their earnest application to me, and my being willing to promote a little subscription for their relief, provided it meet with her approbation.'

'The easiest thing in the world,' cried Miss Diana Parker, who happened to be calling on them at the moment. 'All said and done, in less time than you have been talking of it now. — And while you are on the subject of subscriptions, Mary, I will thank you to mention a very melancholy case to Lady Denham, which has been represented to me in the most affecting terms. — There is a poor woman in Worcestershire, whom some friends of mine are exceedingly interested about, and I have undertaken to collect whatever I can for her. If you would mention the circumstance to Lady Denham! — Lady Denham *can* give, if she is properly attacked — and I look upon her to be the sort of person who, when once she is prevailed on to undraw her purse, would as readily give ten guineas as five. And therefore, if you find her in a giving mood, you might as well speak in favour of another charity which I, and a few more, have very much at heart — the establishment of a charitable repository at Burton on Trent. — And then, — there is the family of the poor man who was hung last assizes at York, though we really *have* raised the sum we wanted for putting them all out, yet if you *can* get a guinea from her on their behalf, it may as well be done.'[21]

'My dear Diana!' exclaimed Mrs. Parker. 'I could no more mention these things to Lady Denham than I could fly.'

'Where's the difficulty? — I wish I could go with you myself — but in five minutes I must be at Mrs. Griffiths's — to encourage Miss Lambe in taking her first dip. She is so frightened, poor thing, that I promised to come and keep up her spirits, and go in the machine with her if she wished it — and, as soon as that is over, I must hurry home, for Susan is to have leeches at one o'clock, which will be a three hours' business — therefore I really have not a moment to spare — besides that (between ourselves) I ought to be in bed myself at this present time, for I am hardly able to stand — and when the leeches have done, I dare say we shall both go to our rooms for the rest of the day.'

'I am sorry to hear it, indeed; but if this is the case I hope Arthur will come to us.'

'If Arthur takes my advice, he will go to bed too, for, if he stays up by himself, he will certainly eat and drink more than he ought; but you see, Mary, how impossible it is for me to go with you to Lady Denham's.'

'Upon second thoughts, Mary,' said her husband, 'I will not trouble you to speak about the Mullins's. I will take an opportunity of seeing Lady Denham myself. I know how little it suits you to be pressing matters upon a mind at all unwilling.'

His application thus withdrawn, his sister could say no more in support of hers, which was his object, as he felt all their impropriety and all the certainty of their ill effect upon his own better claim.

Mrs. Parker was delighted at this release, and set off very happy with her friend and her little girl on this walk to Sanditon House. It was a close, misty morning, and, when they reached the brow of the hill, they could not for some time make out what sort of carriage it was which they saw coming up. It appeared at different moments to be everything from the gig to the phaeton, from one horse to four; and just as they were concluding in favour of a tandem, little Mary's young eyes distinguished the coachman and she eagerly called out, ''Tis Uncle Sidney, Mama, it is indeed.'

And so it proved. Mr. Sidney Parker driving his servant in a very neat carriage was soon opposite to them, and they all stopped for a few minutes.

The manners of the Parkers were always pleasant among themselves, and it was a very friendly meeting between Sidney and his sister-in-law, who was most kindly taking it for granted that he was on his way to Trafalgar House.

This he declined, however. 'He was just come from Eastbourne, proposing to spend two or three days, as it might happen, at Sanditon, but the hotel must be his quarters. He was expecting to be joined there by a friend or two.'

The rest was common enquiries and remarks, with kind notice of little Mary, and a very well-bred bow and proper address to Miss Heywood on her being named to him — and they parted, to meet again within a few hours.

Sidney Parker was about seven or eight and twenty, very good-looking, with a decided air of ease and fashion and a lively countenance. This adventure afforded agreeable discussion for some time. Mrs. Parker entered into all her husband's joy on the occasion, and exulted in the credit which Sidney's arrival would give to the place.

The road to Sanditon House was a broad, handsome, planted approach between fields, and conducting at the end of a quarter of a mile through second gates into the grounds, which though not extensive had all the beauty and respectability which an abundance of very fine timber could give. These entrance gates were so much in a corner of the grounds or paddock, so near one of its boundaries, that an outside fence was at first almost pressing on the road, till an angle here and a curve there threw them to a better distance.

The fence was a proper park paling in excellent condition; with clusters of fine elms, or rows of old thorns following its line almost everywhere. *Almost* must be stipulated, for there were vacant spaces, and, through one of these, Charlotte, as soon as they entered the enclosure, caught a glimpse over the pales of something white and womanish in the field on the other side; it was a something which immediately brought Miss Brereton into her head, and stepping to the pales, she saw indeed — and very decidedly, in spite of the mist — Miss Brereton seated, not far before her, at the foot of the bank which sloped down from the outside of the paling and which a narrow path seemed to skirt along; Miss Brereton seated, apparently very composedly — and Sir Edward Denham by her side.

They were sitting so near each other and appeared so closely engaged in gentle conversation that Charlotte instantly felt she had nothing to do but to step back again, and say not a word. Privacy was certainly their object. It could not but strike her rather unfavourably with regard to Clara; but hers was a situation which must not be judged with severity.

She was glad to perceive that nothing had been discerned by Mrs. Parker; if Charlotte had not been considerably the tallest of the two, Miss Brereton's white ribbons might not have fallen within the ken of *her* more observant eyes. Among other points of moralising reflection which the sight of this tête à tête produced, Charlotte could not but think of the extreme difficulty which secret lovers must have in finding a proper spot for their stolen interviews. Here perhaps they had thought themselves so perfectly secure from observation! — the whole field open before them — a steep bank and pales never crossed by the foot of man at their back — and a great thickness of air, in aid. Yet, here, she had seen them. They were really ill-used.

The house was large and handsome; two servants appeared, to admit them, and everything had a suitable air of property and order. Lady Denham valued herself upon her liberal establishment, and had great enjoyment in the order and importance of her style of living.

They were shown into the usual sitting room, well-proportioned and well-furnished, though it was furniture rather originally good and extremely well kept than new or showy, and, as Lady Denham was not there, Charlotte had leisure to look about, and to be told by Mrs. Parker that the whole length portrait of a stately gentleman, which, placed over the mantelpiece, caught the eye immediately, was the picture of Sir Harry Denham, and that one among many miniatures in another part of the room, little conspicuous, represented Mr. Hollis.

Poor Mr. Hollis! It was impossible not to feel him hardly used; to be obliged to stand back in his own house and see the best place by the fire constantly occupied by Sir Harry Denham.

Endnotes

1   *Sanditon* is full of long journeys in the South of England in
    different types of carriage. The hackney – or hack – carriages
    were hired for a specific trip of the sort Mr. Parker and his
    sisters take from London and Hampshire to the Sussex coast.
    Since roads were often poor, accidents were frequent (and
    were handy plot devices). Austen mocks the use in her teenage
    spoof, *Love and Freindship*, where an overturned carriage kills
    the two heroes, 'most elegantly attired but weltering in their
    blood'. In *Northanger Abbey*, Catherine and the Allens travel
    to Bath without any 'lucky overturn to introduce them to
    the hero'.

2   Battle is a small town, 8 miles from Hastings, commem-
    orating the battle of 1066. Hailsham, mentioned below, is a
    market town 13 miles south west of Battle and 10 miles north
    of Eastbourne. The Weald lies between two chalk uplands,
    the North and South Downs. Austen usually writes 'country'
    for 'county', as here. The *Morning Post* was a London daily
    aimed at the rich and genteel, listing arrivals and departures of
    fashionable people to spas and resorts; the *Kentish Gazette* was
    a bi-weekly local paper. Both advertised goods and services.
    Willingden is as fictional as Sanditon.

3   Economic discussion runs through *Sanditon*. See Introductory
    Essay.

4   'Truth' by William Cowper (1731-1800) contrasts the witty,
    sceptical philosopher Voltaire with a simple countrywoman

who, with her Bible, knows 'A truth the brilliant Frenchman never knew'.

5 Austen is satirising contemporary medical jargon. She actually wrote 'anti-sceptic', possibly alluding to the Parkers' lack of scepticism, but most likely this is just a misspelling.

6 A spa or resort library loaned books and sold accessories and knick- knacks. In *Pride and Prejudice* Lydia Bennet in the Brighton library sees 'such beautiful ornaments as made her quite wild'. Library subscribers would sign a register, which thus became a record of visitors. Looking into it, Mr. Parker is disappointed to find the list of newcomers consisting of low-ranking naval officers and untitled families.

7 Lady Denham's initial £30,000 is similar to the expected fortune of the substantial heiress Emma in *Emma*. A woman's money customarily passed to a husband on marriage; in return she would, if widowed, have a jointure, an income for life, while the main estate went to the male heir. On her second marriage, however, Lady Denham took legal steps to avoid her own and her first husband's money passing directly to her second husband and his heir.

8 The *cottage orné* was a dwelling erected by the gentry in imitation of the rustic cottage of the poor and copying some elements of the natural world. It was usually irregular, spacious, comfortable and very picturesque. The fashion started in the late eighteenth century and continued into the nineteenth. The summer season for sea resorts tended to end in October.

9 Gentlemen used to build manor houses in sheltered valleys, as the ancestral Parkers had done. Mr. Parker's new house is on

a hill to catch the now fashionable sea view. When the great naval battle of Trafalgar was won against the French in 1805, national enthusiasm caused the naming of many streets and houses in commemoration; in 1815, it was superseded in the popular mind by the land victory of Waterloo which ended the long French and Napoleonic Wars.

10   The white frocks, harp and painting stool are fashionable accoutrements of young leisured ladies seeking husbands, and beyond the need or means of the country labourers and fisher-people originally inhabiting the coastal villages.

11   Bathing machines, closed wooden or canvas-sided carriages pulled by horses into the sea, were first introduced either in Margate or in the northern resort of Scarborough.

12   'West Indians' were usually (white) British merchants or planters who had made fortunes in the West Indies. They and their families were often rich and supposedly of uncontrolled temperament because of living in a tropical climate. This characteristic is given to 'mad' Bertha in *Jane Eyre*.

13   *Camilla, or, a Picture of Youth* (1796) by Frances Burney was highly praised in *Northanger Abbey*. When she first read the book, young Jane Austen described herself as 'just like Camilla' who is 17 and who overspends on a visit to Tunbridge Wells. Charlotte is older and more prudent.

14   Asses' milk was considered closer than cows' to human milk, so better for a weak constitution, especially for asthmatics and sufferers from TB. The chamber horse, which Lady Denham offers for hire, was an exercise chair simulating the effect of riding indoors, rather like an exercise bicycle today.

15   Privately owned vehicles included the modest gig, a two-wheeled open carriage with a single horse. The more expensive tandem was a two-wheeled carriage with two horses harnessed one behind the other; and the phaeton was a four-wheeled open carriage drawn by two horses.

16   Sir Edward depicts himself as a man of fashionable sensibility, admirer of the approved Romantic and gothic literature of the day, about which he appears to know little. Before the advent of the more exotic and self-dramatising Lord Byron, Walter Scott was the most famous Romantic poet. The quotation about woman comes from his *Marmion: A Tale of Flodden Field*, and about feelings from *The Lady of the Lake*. The Scottish Robert Burns was celebrated as a rustic, self-taught genius, notorious for his promiscuous love life, to which Charlotte refers disapprovingly. He wrote many poems to Mary Campbell as his 'Highland Mary'. William Wordsworth, Thomas Campbell – the quoted lines are from his *The Pleasures of Hope* – and James Montgomery were all famous at the time; of the three, only Wordsworth is much read now. Romanticism raised poetic geniuses above other men and allowed them to judge themselves by different moral standards; the more prosaic, commonsensical Charlotte rejects the idea, as did Jane Austen. Charlotte enjoys imposing literature on mundane life, transforming Clara into a gothic heroine, but, as her response to *Camilla* and her attitude to Burns show, literary fiction does not impose on her. She likes quotations to be accurate.

17   Income for the more prosperous classes came from land or investments in government stocks or funds. The Heywoods live on an inherited farming estate but Mr Heywood also goes

to London twice a year to collect his dividend payments. The Parker brothers all have inherited income though the eldest received the family estate and seems the only one feeling a need to work. With the end of the long French wars, officers were retained on much reduced pay.

18 Sir Edward is as foolish about novels as about poetry. His views contrast with those of Jane Austen, who, in *Northanger Abbey*, praises novels 'in which the greatest powers of the mind are displayed'. The novel that has most influenced Sir Edward is Samuel Richardson's masterpiece, *Clarissa, or the History of a Young Lady*, published half a century earlier in 1748. It depicts the aristocratic Lovelace abducting and raping the virtuous heroine. Richardson intended a moral message in his powerful display of male cunning and female suffering and was appalled to discover many readers charmed by the wit and humour of the villainous Lovelace. According to James Edward Austen-Leigh, Jane Austen's 'knowledge of Richardson's works was such as no-one is likely again to acquire', and Richardson was always a strong influence on her dialogue and psychological plotting; however, her depiction of silly Sir Edward as a fan of Richardson, even if for an absurd reason, suggests her unquestioning admiration had cooled by this time.

19 The scientific study of the body.

20 Girls showing off their genteel accomplishments, such as singing, playing the piano or harp, sketching, painting, embroidering and dancing, to attract a good offer of marriage.

21 A charitable repository was a precursor of today's charity shop, a place where donated objects could be sold to benefit the poor. The assizes were court sessions for different regions:

crimes carrying the penalty of hanging included theft of even small items, highway robbery and forgery. 'Putting children out' was setting them up for life through apprenticeships, which required initial payment. Burton on Trent and York are very far from the south coast of England.

Note on the text

The text is based on the transcription prepared by Linda Bree for *Later Manuscript Works,* edited by Janet Todd and Linda Bree as part of the Cambridge Edition of Jane Austen. Many thanks to Cambridge University Press for allowing use of its text. I have made a few minor alterations to render it more accessible to a modern reader (in doing so, I have had to sacrifice its appearance as a draft work in process). In manuscripts, punctuation mainly by dashes was common, especially, it was often noted, in works by women writers. These dashes were usually reduced in a printed text; so I have eliminated some, retaining them mainly to suggest rushed or jumbled thoughts. I have added paragraphing and modernised spelling of a few words such as 'ankle' and 'stayed', and I have expanded abbreviations which were common in writing but less so in a printed text.

The original manuscript is held in King's College, Cambridge.

Anna Lefroy to Andrew Davies: Continuations of Sanditon

Most Austen novels declare their plot before they reach 24,000 words, but *Sanditon* leaves its story wide open. Perhaps for this reason there are fewer continuations than might be expected – until, of course, the post-millennium fevered spin-off industry when, through self-publishing, vanity presses and fanvids, boundaries are forsaken, and the works of the megastar Jane Austen are continued, adapted, appropriated, exploited and flamboyantly enjoyed by millions.

There is some authoritative precedent for providing characters with afterlives. In the *Memoir*, her nephew James Edward Austen-Leigh wrote of Jane Austen:

> She would, if asked, tell us many little particulars about the subsequent career of some of her people. In this traditionary way we learned that Miss Steele never succeeded in catching the Doctor; that Kitty Bennet was satisfactorily married to a clergyman near Pemberley, while Mary obtained nothing higher than one of her uncle Philips' clerks, and was content to be considered a star in the society of Meriton; that the 'considerable sum' given by Mrs. Norris to William Price was one pound; that Mr. Woodhouse survived his daughter's

marriage, and kept her and Mr. Knightley from settling at Donwell, about two years; and that the letters
placed by Frank Churchill before Jane Fairfax, which
she swept away unread, contained the word 'pardon'.
Of the good people in *Northanger Abbey* and *Persuasion*
we know nothing more than what is written: for before
those works were published their author had been taken
away from us, and all such amusing communications
had ceased for ever.

Below are descriptions of three early continuations of
Sanditon and a mention of some others. The main decision
of authors – invariably concerned more with romance than
with satire – is whether to let Clara Brereton remain as
virtuous as she is beautiful or to make her a sly schemer.

Anna Lefroy, *Sanditon*. Anna Austen, later Lefroy, inherited Jane Austen's manuscript from her aunt Cassandra, so
her continuation must date from after 1845. Of her relation
with the Austen text, Anna wrote, 'The truth is, I am getting fond of Mr. Parker. The other members of the Parker
family . . . were certainly suggested by conversations which
passed between Aunt Jane & me during the time that she
was writing this story' – although some critics suggest
Anna probably exaggerates the amount of discussion.

The unfinished continuation, about the length of Austen's
original, de-emphasises the eccentric characters and invents

a rather un-Austen villain, who is Sidney Parker's friend as well as being associated with the past of the impecunious Sir Edward: he is also a political agent. Charlotte instinctively dislikes him. Charlotte and Sidney seem destined for each other, and Mr. Parker is most likely heading for financial misfortune, since visitors to Sanditon do not materialise. Possibly he would be rescued by brother Sidney, who has more scepticism than his siblings and who has not speculated with his inheritance.

By the time the continuation trails off, little has happened in the resort, except that Mr. Parker has hired two donkeys for the beach, using two naughty Sunday School boys as minders, and Miss Lambe, torpid because of her 'Creole nature', is persuaded to ride one.

The main tale is followed by fragments of the backstory of Clara Brereton, her feckless family and her rejection as nursery maid because of her prettiness. Lacking a proper Christian upbringing, she has become 'cold, calculating & selfish'.

Although by the 1840s and '50s Anna Lefroy was a modest published author, perhaps she was discouraged in her continuing of *Sanditon* by coming so close to the writing of Jane Austen. She remarked of her aunt's work beside her own: 'There seems to me just the same difference as between real Lace, & Imitation.'

Anna's continuation is transcribed in Mary Gaither Marshall's *Jane Austen's* Sanditon (1983).

Alice Cobbett's *Somehow Lengthened: A Development of 'Sanditon'* (1932) begins with the characters and basic storyline of *Sanditon,* but uses none of Austen's writing and more or less abandons the Parkers. The sensational plot is sometimes close to Austen's skit, 'Plan of a Novel', which includes the suggestion for the heroine: 'Often carried away by the anti-hero'.

In Cobbett's work, the nefarious Sir Edward abducts Clara Brereton with the help of smugglers; Charlotte rescues her and then, through the good offices of a real (rather than 'mean-spirited') great lady, Clara is persuaded to marry Sir Edward on the grounds that marrying without love is better for a poor girl than remaining dependent on a rich old lady's whims. Young Miss Lambe, here an octoroon accompanied by a black 'mammy', unfortunately falls for Sir Edward, but regains happiness at the idea of returning to Barbados from chilly England. Sidney Parker marries Miss Denham and Charlotte marries a man introduced on the last page, an echo of the comic ending of *Northanger Abbey*.

Marie Dobbs, *Sanditon*, by Jane Austen and Another Lady (1975). This work prints passages from Austen's fragment, then continues with no break. It resembles Georgette Heyer's sort of romantic comedy and drops the broad satire on medicine and invalid tourism of the Austen original. It avoids any discussion of speculation and capitalism, leaving the town of Sanditon at the end to continue much as it was, neither collapsing nor especially flourishing.

Two new characters arrive, friends of the witty, vain Sidney Parker (here, resembling *Emma*'s Frank Churchill), and, although Charlotte spends most of the novel assuming Sir Edward and Clara are about to elope, one of these new characters turns out to be Clara's intended partner in elopement. Unaware of this fact, Sir Edward arranges his abduction of Clara, but, failing to find her, abducts Charlotte instead, only to discover that he has galloped with her towards her own home. Sir Edward and his sister are left out in the cold, while others pair up: Clara goes to Bengal with her lover; Sidney Parker will marry Charlotte; and Miss Lambe and Arthur Parker unite over a shared interest in shells and seaweed.

Rebecca Baldwin, *A Sanditon Quadrille* (1981) uses Austen's work simply as background, noting 'the irresistible lure of a Regency resort as the natural setting for romantic tangling and untangling'.

Julia Barrett, *Jane Austen's Charlotte: Her Fragment of a Last Novel, Completed* (2002) continues with Austen's characters, adding many new ones. The plot is melodrama rather than social comedy, with smuggling and gambling being at the centre.

Reginald Hill, *A Cure for All Diseases* (UK); *The Price of Butcher's Meat* (US) (2008) transforms *Sanditon* into a contemporary crime-fiction of emails, blogs and traditional narrative. It begins with Tom Parker's accident in his car while seeking a complementary therapist for the Yorkshire resort which he is resurrecting to compete against cheap Mediterranean package holidays. The detective Andrew Dalziel is recuperating there when Lady Denham (here named Daphne – she is Sarah Wilhelmina in Cobbett) is murdered in a way suggestive of roasting pig – much of her money comes from 'Hog' Hollis's ham freezer packs. Charlie, a student and guest of the Parkers, feels she is in a Miss Marple film as she helps solve the case.

Helen Marshall, 'Sanditon' (2012) is a short story set in London. In it the full text of a finished *Sanditon* appears under the skin in the neck of a modern book editor. We never read the manuscript.

Carrie Bebris, *The Suspicion at Sanditon (Or, the Disappearance of Lady Denham)* (2015) uses *Pride and Prejudice*'s Darcys as detectives. They are drawn in when they dine with Lady Denham, who then disappears; the Darcys must solve the case. Soon Susan Parker also disappears. Were the women abducted or killed?

The blog *Welcome to Sanditon* (2013) is a spin-off produced by Pemberley Digital. Some of the characters from the popular *Lizzie Bennet Diaries* appear here: for example, Gigi Darcy spends the summer in Sanditon, California, testing Domino, a new video-conferencing software produced by her brother's company.

In other forms of entertainment, there is Chris Brindle's *Jane Austen's Sanditon: The-Film-of-the-Play,* using the Austen and Lefroy texts. This is a rehearsed reading with music of the two-act play Brindle wrote in 2014 when he possessed the Lefroy manuscript. Based on Brindle's stage completion a pop/rock, actor/musician musical called '200 Years Later' will be recorded in July 2019.

A two-hour film from Fluidity Films using Marie Dobbs's completion was proposed some time ago, but no release date has been set.

An ITV eight-part mini-series of *Sanditon* is being produced by Red Planet pictures, with Andrew Davies's screenplay. Its central action will concern the edgy relationship between a spirited, unconventional Charlotte and a charming Sidney Parker. The new ending is not publicly known, but it would shock viewers if the series did not contain nude bathing and a colourful visit to the West Indies.

Why not make your own version? Or, ignoring fandom and film, live contentedly in Jane Austen's original resort, taking after-dinner tea in Trafalgar House and listening with one ear to the burbling of Sir Edward and Diana Parker.

Further reading

Those wanting to find *Sanditon* in its manuscript or trans-
literated form should consult *The Cambridge Edition of the
Works of Jane Austen: Later Manuscripts* (2008) and *Jane
Austen's Fiction Manuscripts Digital Edition*. For more
information on Jane Austen's life and times, see the many
biographies, especially Deirdre Le Faye's *Jane Austen: A
Family Record* (2004), Paula Byrne's *The Real Jane Austen:
A Life in Small Things* (2013) and Lucy Worsley's *Jane
Austen at Home* (2017); for specific details of Henry Austen,
see E. J. Clery's *Jane Austen, the Banker's Sister* (2017).
John Wiltshire's *Jane Austen and the Body* (1992) is invalu-
able for treatment of Jane Austen and sickness and Edward
Copeland's *Women Writing about Money: Women's Fiction
in England 1790–1820* (1995) for discussion of Austen and
money. For the claims of Worthing, see Antony Edmonds's
Jane Austen's Worthing: The Real Sanditon (2013) and for
resorts in general, Brian Southam's 'Jane Austen beside the
Seaside: An Introduction', *Persuasions*, no. 32, (2010) and
David Selwyn's *Jane Austen and Leisure* (1999).

For academic discussion of *Sanditon* as manuscript text,
see Brian Southam's *Jane Austen's Literary Manuscripts*
(1964), Kathryn Sutherland's *Jane Austen's Textual Lives*
(2005) and the Introduction to *Later Manuscripts. Persuasions*

On-Line, Vol. 38 no. 2, ed. Anne Toner has critical, cultural and textual articles by Sutherland, Clery, Michelle Levy, Julian Banister, Jane Darcy, Amanda E. Himes, Akiko Takei, Margaret Case, Kathryn Davies, Kathy Justice Gentile, Natalie DeVaull Robichaud, Clara Tuite, Olivia Ferguson, Joe Bray, Anne Toner, Peter Sabor, Maria Clara Pivato Biajoli and Katie Halsey. *Sanditon* is discussed in sections of Tony Tanner's *Jane Austen* (1986), Clara Tuite's *Romantic Austen: Sexual Politics and the Literary Canon* (2002), D. A. Miller's *Jane Austen, or The Secret of Style* (2003), John Mullan's *What Matters in Jane Austen* (2012) and Devoney Looser's *The Making of Jane Austen* (2017).

Quotations in the Introductory Essay are from Deirdre le Faye's revised edition of *Jane Austen's Letters* (2011), Peter Sabor's edition of *Juvenilia* (2013) in the *Cambridge Edition of the Works of Jane Austen* and from Kathryn Sutherland's edition of *A Memoir of Jane Austen* by J. E. Austen-Leigh (2002).

List of Illustrations

LIST OF ILLUSTRATIONS

Acknowledgements

Anyone working in the exciting, crowded field of Jane Austen texts and criticism will owe thanks to many wonderful scholars and readers. Over the years, I have had lively debates and conversations on Austen's fiction and letters with fellow enthusiasts throughout the world. I owe special thanks to Linda Bree, Diana Birchall, Robert Clark, Gillian Dow, Devoney Looser and Peter Sabor. I am hugely grateful to Deirdre Le Faye, always so generous with information and advice.

For this edition of Sanditon, I would like to thank Derek Hughes and John Gardner and, above all, the very patient and skilful Art Petersen for assistance with the illustrations. I owe thanks to Rosemary Gray, Lindsay Nash, Sarah Wasley, David Wightman and Jeremy Hopes for work on producing the book.

My main thanks must go to Katherine Bright-Holmes for her enthusiasm and encouragement at every stage of this project.